Success in
Pre-Paid Legal

—the proven system that never fails!

Paul J. Meyer and Kevin Rhea

insight *publishing group*

Tulsa, Oklahoma

Success in Pre-Paid Legal by Paul J. Meyer and Kevin Rhea
Published by Insight Publishing Group
8801 S. Yale, Suite 410
Tulsa, OK 74137
918-493-1718

1st printing: 20,000

How to Order: Single copies and bulk orders can be made through Video*Plus*:
- Order online at www.ppltools-videoplus.com
- Phone orders: 1-800-388-3884
- Fax orders: 1-940-497-9799
- Mail orders to: Video*Plus* Inc. 200 Swisher Road Lake Dallas, TX 75065

ISBN: 1-930027-51-6
Library of Congress catalog card number: 2002100414

Printed in the United States of America

Table of Contents

Acknowledgments

Foreword by Harland C. Stonecipher

Preface by Kevin Rhea

Introduction by Paul J. Meyer

PART I—THE SHORTEST ROUTE TO YOUR SUCCESS

1	The shortest route to your success	17
2	7 foundational qualities of the top producers	29
3	Preparing for a phenomenal start	45

PART II—STARTING SUCCESSFULLY

4	The Game Plan interview	65
5	Your goals on paper	81
6	Your Plan of Action	91
7	Your final preparations	105

PART III—TAKING ACTION TOWARD YOUR SUCCESS

8	Take aim, take action!	121
9	Long-distance sales and recruiting	139
10	Face-to-face sales and recruiting	155
11	Follow through to follow up	173

PART IV—TRAINING FOR CONTINUED SUCCESS

12	Prospecting	187
13	Presenting	207
14	Getting referrals	219
15	Recruiting	233
16	Duplicating	251

Conclusion

Reference Information for Pre-Paid Legal

Acknowledgments

We would like to thank the many top producers in Pre-Paid Legal who contributed to the proven system outlined in the following pages and who took of their time to help make this book a reality. Each of these top producers has earned anywhere from $100,000 to $1,000,000 per year and has been with the company for at least three years.

The top producers and top trainers in Pre-Paid Legal who shared their many years of knowledge and experience include:

- Kathy Aaron
- Frank and Theresa AuCoin
- Mark Brown
- Brian Carruthers
- Bill Carter and Linda Diesel
- Michael Clouse
- Kelvin and Yvetta Collins
- Michael Dorsey
- Alan Erdlee
- Steve Fleming
- John and Elizabeth Gardner
- Bill and Annette Hamilton
- Craig Hepner
- John Hoffman
- Mike Melia
- Steve Melia
- Jeff Olson
- Ed Parker
- Denise Patrick
- Mark Riches
- Dave Savula
- Darnell Self
- Patrick Shaw
- Ken Smith and Patti Ross
- Larry Smith
- Wilburn Smith
- Dan Stammen
- Dennis Windsor
- Tom Wood
- Eric Worre

Foreword
by Harland C. Stonecipher

"Equal justice under law" sounds good, the only problem is that it isn't true. The fact is you get as much justice as you can afford. In today's marketplace, justice is on par with suits, cars, and homes—you can buy it—and the more money you have the better version you can get!

This ought not to be! Everyone deserves justice, but understandably, not everyone can afford it . . . until now.

With a Pre-Paid Legal membership, you have the peace of mind **and** the protection that comes from having one of the top-ranked law firms in the nation on your side!

I've read thousands of stories of people who have used their Pre-Paid Legal membership and received the justice they deserve:

- ◆ like the family that now has a Will in place, deciding what they want instead of letting the state decide
- ◆ like the salesman who had his speeding ticket reduced so his insurance didn't go any higher
- ◆ like the lady heading to a pharmacist at 2:30 a.m. for child who was pulled over and about to be searched, but when she called her lawyer, the police officer apologized and drove away
- ◆ like the retiree who was charged with accidental vehicular manslaughter and had a top-ranked lawyer represent him, clear him, and not charge him a dime more than what he paid for his membership

- like the 8 teenagers who were detained by police late one night, but when 2 of the 8 produced Pre-Paid Legal cards, only those 2 were immediately released
- like the couple about to lease a car who decided to fax the agreement to their lawyer—and saved $1,200 by the lawyer spotting "hidden costs"
- like the disabled man who had his insurance reinstated with the help of his lawyer, along with $15,000 retroactively

There are countless stories and each one makes my very proud of what we do at Pre-Paid Legal Services, Inc. Imagine if everyone had justice!

There is something else that makes my heart beat with excitement and that is seeing people become financially free through the business opportunity that Pre-Paid Legal presents. I have seen lives changed, children attend colleges they only once dreamed of attending, dream homes purchased and paid off, single-parents provide handsomely for their family, debts canceled, and old dreams re-awakened! It's amazing to see and even more amazing to experience.

I want more millionaires to come from Pre-Paid Legal Services, Inc. than any other company in history. We are on the way. For you to get there, you will have to begin where every other Associate began—at the beginning. From there, following the proven system that other top producers have followed, there is nothing in your way that you should not be able to overcome.

That is what *Success in Pre-Paid Legal* is all about. Paul J. Meyer and Kevin Rhea have done an incredible job detailing the steps you need to take to get you where you want to go. The proven system they write about has been tried and tested. It works, it produces, and it's simple.

With the experience and advice from 30 of Pre-Paid Legal's top producers compressed into this one book, I expect to be shaking your hand some time very soon—on stage!

Congratulations for helping change history and congratulations on your future!

Harland C. Stonecipher

Preface by Kevin Rhea

Imagine having a detailed map to success in Pre-Paid Legal that everyone (including those who won't stop and ask for directions) could successfully follow. The amount of time, effort, and money saved would be incredible, possibly even incalculable! If such a map existed, I would spare no expense to get it, knowing full well that success was imminent.

You are holding one such map in your hands!

This book is based on the advice, wisdom, and experience of 30 of the top producers and top trainers in Pre-Paid Legal and truly is a map to your success. These top producers are some of the company's top money earners who have received recognition for earning anywhere from $100,000 to $500,000 to even $1,000,000 per year.

Wrapped around this core training for success in Pre-Paid Legal are the sales, personal development, training, and management secrets of Paul J. Meyer, an individual who has been in the success motivation, leadership, and training business for more than 50 years. His materials have been sold in numerous countries and languages for a combined total of more than two billion dollars!

From A to Z, what you need to do to succeed in Pre-Paid Legal is clearly outlined in the following chapters. Add in your hard work and commitment to the process and you are well on your way to reaching your dreams.

Congratulations on your imminent success!

Kevin Rhea,
President of L-K Marketing Group

Introduction
by Paul J. Meyer

When I started selling as a profession, I was 19 years old and fresh out of the military. I was fresh out of college as well, having quit after only 90 days. Schools were overcrowded (World War II was over and everyone was going to college on the GI Bill), getting classes was difficult, and the pace of learning was excruciatingly slow. When the counselor said I could not read all the material on my own and take the tests when I was ready, I packed my bags and left.

What I wanted to do was sell life insurance. I had sold *Ladies Home Journal* and *Liberty Magazine* when I was 12 or 13, but the life insurance industry was different—you had to first be hired by a company, and I was having trouble getting hired.

After filling out applications and knocking on the doors of 57 different life insurance companies, I still didn't have a job. With no college degree, they quickly disregarded me. They never once asked what I could do, how motivated I was, how much common sense I had, or anything about my work ethic. A judgmental attitude prevailed!

After 57 "no thank yous" in a row, I finally found a job with a life insurance company, but three short weeks later they fired me claiming that I was too shy, introverted, and simply not cut out for the profession. I protested, explaining that I had the desire, ability, and passion to be the best in the business and that I was just learning. They didn't listen and they didn't care.

I was able to find another job selling weekly premiums to a market that nobody else wanted to sell to (that was why I got the job).

Moving into the big league

Two years later, after leading the company (and the nation!) in the sale of weekly premiums, I felt I was ready to sell ordinary or whole insurance—where the premiums were mailed to the company and I didn't have to go out and personally collect 10¢ or 50¢ every week from my clients!

An insurance company starting a new branch in Columbus, Georgia gave me my chance, but after 9 months of selling ordinary life insurance, *my average monthly income was a mere $87 a month!* Things did not look good on the outside, but on the inside, things were falling into place. My attitude, belief in myself, belief in my product, and level of expectation were unstoppable! I kept my Million Dollar Personal Success Plan in front of me at all times. It read:

1. *Crystallize your thinking.*
2. *Develop a plan for achieving your goal and a deadline for its attainment.*
3. *Develop a sincere desire for the things you want in life.*
4. *Develop supreme confidence in yourself and your own abilities.*
5. *Develop a dogged determination to follow through on your plan regardless of obstacles, criticism or circumstances or what other people say, think, or do.*

I knew that if I stayed with it long enough, I would eventually reach my goals. Every day I was learning, watching, planning, practicing, and getting better. My closing average continued to improve as I acquired the selling skills I needed and in my 10th month my income jumped to $3000! (In 1950-dollars, that would be about $30,000 today!) Six months later I qualified to become the youngest salesman ever to attain membership in the Million Dollar Round Table!

The following year I sold almost four million dollars worth of insurance. I went on to out-perform every salesman I laid eyes on and won every sales competition I entered in every insurance company I worked for.

That was then, this is now

From those days in life insurance, many things have changed. I went on to start more than 100 different businesses (65% of which have failed) and, among other things, wrote 24 full-length courses and programs in leadership development and management training that sold extremely well.

But in many ways, nothing has changed. The principles for success, like possessing a positive attitude, proper time management, setting goals, being disciplined, not taking "no" for an answer, etc., will always remain the same. Only the people and the industries change.

When I started selling weekly premium insurance, I was handed several applications, a sample life insurance policy, and dropped off in a neighborhood 4 miles from the office. ***That was the extent of my training!*** I had never even seen an insurance policy before, let alone been taught about knowing my product, making a presentation, or asking for referrals.

I collected my wits and realized that standing there wouldn't sell anything. I quickly read the policy and then walked to the closest house. After I knocked and the door opened, I took off my hat and politely stated my business, adding that this was the first house I'd called on and that I'd never sold any insurance in my life. She invited me in and we looked over the policy together—and she bought it! It was my first sale! I asked her who lived next door and she told me. Then I asked her if she would introduce me to her neighbor. The first neighbor bought as well, as did the next and the next! I was the #1 producer in the agency from my first day!

Thankfully this trial-by-fire approach is no longer standard protocol, especially in Pre-Paid Legal. Yes, it is important to get your feet wet by jumping in and getting started, but starting off in a sink-or-swim position scares many people out of what could be a very promising career. What most people need is a replicable, black and white, 1-2-3, A-B-C, step-by-step process on how to succeed in Pre-Paid Legal.

That is the reason for this book!

Helping you get where you want to go

Not everyone who sees the potential within Pre-Paid Legal will have experience in sales, marketing, public speaking, or team management. I know of an individual in Pre-Paid Legal who had no sales experience, no insurance experience, and no network marketing experience. It took him four months to make his first sale!

Today, however, John Biro is making a six-figure income in Pre-Paid Legal and enjoying his business and time with his family like never before.

He got there slowly while others get there quickly, but the point is, he got there!

Whatever your style, perceived ability, experience, or background, you have just as much of a chance to achieve your dreams as those who have achieved theirs. I should know. I grew up the son of an immigrant and picking seasonal fruit in the orchards of California. We were never financially well off and lived in a garage for 10 years! My high school may not have voted me the most likely to succeed, but I chose myself as the most likely to succeed—**and I choose you!**

You can achieve your dreams, accomplish your goals, and do the impossible. Sure, it will take time, effort, and determination, but don't let that stop you.

With Pre-Paid Legal, I believe you have the best business opportunity in the world. Pre-Paid Legal is a solid company (being in existence since 1972) that has, among other things:

- no debt
- tens of millions of cash in the bank
- consistently profitable quarters
- a solid infrastructure
- the best business model of any marketing company ever!

The future of Pre-Paid Legal is only bright! With statistics showing that 9 out of 10 people have never heard of Pre-Paid Legal, that people are 3 times more likely to need a lawyer than they are to go to the hospital, and that 70% of people do not have a Will, **the need for Pre-Paid Legal is only increasing**. All of these ingredients make Pre-Paid Legal a truly incredible service and opportunity.

Designed with your success in mind

The best news is that you don't have to learn how to market Pre-Paid Legal on your own, the hard way, by trial and error, or by accident. Thirty of the top producers in Pre-Paid Legal have taken the time to share their secrets for success here with you.

Every chapter is packed with step-by-step advice and "how to" training from these top producers, all designed with your success in mind. By applying their proven system, you will know precisely what you need to do to succeed in Pre-Paid Legal. I guarantee it!

Sadly, too many people have tried their own methods of presenting the service, training, recruiting, etc. Some failed to even sell one membership while others sold hundreds in a manner that was not duplicable. Most of these people, hopefully, reached a point where they were dissatisfied with their results "their way" and said, "I'll do it the way I'm taught." *That is where things begin to take off!*

Mark and Renee West, for example, called themselves "puppets" when they started with Pre-Paid Legal. "We did exactly what was proven to work by the people who had already tested the methods," they said. "As long as we remained teachable, we knew we couldn't go wrong." They didn't go wrong and built up a very successful business and are making even bigger plans for the future.

Again, the reason for having the top producers give you their secrets to success with Pre-Paid Legal is so that you can repeat what they have done and reap the same results. It really isn't any more difficult than that.

I wish you tremendous success in Pre-Paid Legal!

PART I

THE SHORTEST
ROUTE TO YOUR SUCCESS

Success in Pre-Paid Legal is a lot like using a hand pump on a well. To get water out, you need consistent action to work the water up from below. If you quit just before the water comes out, the water will drop and you will have to start the process over the next time you return to the pump.

Achieving success in Pre-Paid Legal also comes through consistent action. As your momentum builds through consistent action, it won't be long before success is pouring out of your Pre-Paid Legal business. Then don't stop—pump even faster!

Kevin Rhea, president of L-K Marketing Group

Chapter #1 reveals:

- Why the right attitude precedes success

- How to activate your hidden potential

- The impact of positive expectancy on you and your success

- The shortest route to your success in Pre-Paid Legal

"Justice For All"

THE SHORTEST ROUTE TO YOUR SUCCESS

Before I tell you of three individuals who are succeeding in Pre-Paid Legal, let me first say that the route each took to be successful was vastly different! There are of course more than three routes to find success in Pre-Paid Legal, **but I recommend that you take the shortest one.**

You'll see what I mean . . .

Doug was completely new to sales, but he was quick to recognize that those who were making the kind of money he had always wanted to make must be doing something right. He figured, and correctly so, that to be successful in Pre-Paid Legal, all he needed to do was follow the proven system that the top producers had already set in place. Progress was steady as he began to master the learning curve.

Karon had some sales experience, but her greatest initial asset was her confidence in herself. It allowed her to talk to or call anyone, whether she knew them or not, and ask them to review Pre-Paid Legal. When she followed up and received a "no" or even a few "what in the world do you think you are doing?" from her family and relatives, she kept on going. Progress was consistent and rewarding as she continued to move forward.

Bill was the sales pro who, after leading the sales team at his company for 5 years, was looking for something that would produce a hefty residual income. Pre-Paid Legal fit perfectly within his plan. His progress was rapid as membership sales went through the roof!

Why you joined Pre-Paid Legal

Everybody who becomes an Associate in Pre-Paid Legal does so for a very good reason. It is **their** reason, and that is what makes it so important. They have a dream, a goal, or a desire that they want to see become a reality. Whether it's an additional $500 to $1000 a month or a multiple 6-figure or even 7-figure income, everyone has a reason for joining Pre-Paid Legal.

Whatever your reason, a positive attitude is necessary to see your dream to its completion, and the more positive your attitude, the quicker your dreams come to pass, regardless of how big they might be! The fact of the matter is that each of us has an overall pattern of thinking that is generally either positive or negative. The pattern you choose has four profound effects on your life:

> Secrets of the Top Producers
> "Having the right attitude will bring more success than anything else will."
> -Kevin Rhea, Waco, TX

#1—your attitude affects your belief in your potential for success

A negative attitude causes you to doubt your ability to achieve, while belief in your potential makes you willing to take the necessary action for success.

#2—your attitude determines what you think about facing a challenge

A positive attitude lets you see a challenge as an opportunity rather than a threat.

#3—your attitude determines your confidence

People with negative attitudes have so often thought "I can't . . ." or "I doubt . . ." that belief in their individual potential is non-existent. Each time you act from a positive attitude, your self-confidence is enhanced, your ability to achieve is proven, and you know you can succeed.

#4—your attitude affects how you see opportunity

People who have a negative attitude have buried the ability to see opportunity. A positive attitude, by contrast, opens your eyes to so many opportunities that your challenge becomes which opportunity to choose!

If you have big dreams and big plans, you must also have a positive attitude to back it up. When that attitude is in place, you might even find that your dreams and goals are a little small!

Tap your untapped potential—*and awaken the giant within!*

Libraries are filled with story after story of "stupid" or awkward or poor kids who couldn't pass exams in school or make the team or buy lunch. Yet some way, some how, they went on to great success—great inventions, Olympic gold medals, multi-million dollar foundations, etc. You name it, the

> **Homerun!**
> #1.1—Staying excited about Pre-Paid Legal regardless what others say, think, or do

unexpected has happened! In Pre-Paid Legal, many Associates are doing incredibly well who were once mowing lawns, washing dishes, waiting on tables, or completely unemployed. These people awakened the giant within themselves.

So how did all of these individuals separate themselves from the "average" or less-than-average people around them? The answer is that they made a conscious choice and a conscious decision to do whatever they had to do to tap into their massive, unused potential. Have you tapped into your massive, unused potential?

On the practical level, if you have 20 years of experience in sales or you signed up to become a new Associate with Pre-Paid Legal only days ago, it really makes no difference! Who you are,

> **Homerun!**
> #1.2—Waking up each day without giving mental recognition to the possibility of defeat

what you choose to become, and whether you awaken your giant within—it will always come down to YOU!

Here are four steps you can take to shake your sleeping giant:

#1. Believe in yourself! Believe that you do have a sleeping giant within and an untapped potential, that you are unique and different, and that you can develop and grow and achieve. When you believe in yourself, others will believe in you. They will put their trust in your ideas. They will cooperate with you. And they will receive the same benefits of this positive expectancy from their own experience. Believing in yourself and in your work enables you to multiply your efforts and magnify your results.

#2. *Expect to succeed!* Living life with positive expectancy produces great rewards. Remember, the only limitations you will ever have are those you place on yourself. I wake up each day without giving mental recognition to the possibility of defeat. I expect to succeed! This is my attitude and it affects everything I do, say, or think.

#3. *Visualize yourself succeeding!* Never see yourself as you are now, but only how you would be if you wake up the giant within and develop your hidden potential. That is because you can only be what you visualize yourself being, you can do only what you visualize yourself doing, and you can have only what you visualize yourself having. Each success draws you closer to the mental picture that you have of your new future.

#4. *Get excited about Pre-Paid Legal!* In addition:

 ◆ Get emotionally involved!
 ◆ Become passionate!
 ◆ Feel your adrenaline pump!
 ◆ Become enthusiastic!

I have never seen these four action steps fail to produce! You will forever be a different person when the sleeping giant awakens within you!

You can do this!—*the power of positive expectancy*

More than any other characteristic, quality, or trait of human personality, an attitude of positive expectancy is the companion of success in every achievement, every worthwhile venture, every upward step in human progress, and Pre-Paid Legal!

William James, the founder of American psychology, said, "The one thing that will guarantee the successful conclusion of a doubtful undertaking is faith in the beginning that you can do it."

This faith in the beginning that you can do it is called positive expectancy! The giant within you thrives on positive expectancy, which:

♦ transforms you into a self-starter
♦ pushes you to develop your potential
♦ inspires you to use your imagination and creativity
♦ impels you to take purposeful action
♦ produces determination
♦ forces you to improve and to change
♦ enables you to maintain a positive attitude

> Secrets of the Top Producers
> **"Hang out with positive people."**
> -Ed Parker, Flower Mound, TX

With positive expectancy, you can surpass your prior levels of success and often achieve a great deal more than others who lack this essential quality. There is magic in positive expectancy!

To adopt these beliefs and make them operative in your life, you need:

A. **a no-limitations belief in yourself!** You are unique. Your dreams come from the essence of who you really are.

B. **a no-limitations belief in the potential of other people!** Helping other people recognize their potential and use it meaningfully provides a rich, fulfilling sense of accomplishment. Always encourage others and be willing to give them an opportunity to prove what they can be and what they can do.

C. **a no-limitations belief in potentials and possibilities!** The greatest dreams are yet to be dreamed, the most constructive concepts are yet to be formulated, and the most successful plans are yet to be drawn!

Positive expectancy works! It gives you the power of concentration. By focusing all of your thoughts, plans, and actions on the object of your belief, you 1) define your priorities, 2) block out your obstacles, 3) maintain your enthusiasm, and 4) take responsibility for actions necessary to reach your goal.

At all costs, develop an attitude of positive expectancy. Then when you meet any obstacle or roadblock, you will immediately try again until you get over, under, or through it. Setbacks become temporary—never permanent—because you never stop trying. Positive expectancy also refuses to let what anyone says, thinks, or does discourage you.

> 90% of all success comes from attitude

There is power in positive expectancy. Your job is to harness it for yourself as you begin your journey with Pre-Paid Legal.

This is just the beginning

So what happened to Doug, Karon, and Bill? They are all doing very well in Pre-Paid Legal today, but it wasn't a quick trip for everyone.

Doug methodically plugged away at the learning curve in front of him. He learned the main points of the Pre-Paid Legal presentation by heart, attended every meeting he could, and used his sponsor for 3-way calls all the time. He let the tools do the talking for him because he knew that the more he talked, the less sales he would make.

Slowly but surely his membership sales increased. He even recruited a few better-qualified individuals who are also passionate about Pre-Paid Legal. It took him about 6 months before he was comfortable making a presentation to someone without his sponsor, but he knew it was a vital step for his success. Doug was patient with himself as he grew more confident, primarily because he understood the bright future ahead of him.

Karon's confidence and experience quickly built into a level of enthusiasm that was contagious. She soon recruited several individuals and started helping them toward their dreams. Membership sales from which she earned a commission began to come in from all over North America. Before she knew it, her organization was in 15 states and growing rapidly. She had moments where nothing seemed to click, but she persisted and refused to let one bad day or a long string of "no thank you" responses influence her next presentation. Her

> **Secrets of the Top Producers**
> "When you are blind to discouragement, deaf to the suggestion of defeat, and numb to criticism, you are well on your way to success in Pre-Paid Legal."
> -Paul J. Meyer, Waco, TX

attitude was always positive and it began to reflect in her paycheck. One year into the business and her part-time salary with Pre-Paid Legal equaled her full-time salary, so she fired her boss and went full-time in Pre-Paid Legal!

Bill's entrance into Pre-Paid Legal was certainly fast and furious. His membership sales gained him much recognition his first few months, but his super ability to sell inhibited him from recruiting anyone.

One recruit after another would say, "I can see the value of the membership, but as for me selling it to other people, I could never be as good as you are. Maybe if I was better in sales." It wasn't until he called his sponsor and asked for help did things turn around. He learned that his superb salesmanship was a good quality, but it wasn't duplicable—and if another person couldn't do what he was doing, then they certainly weren't willing to try it. It took him several months to reprogram himself to let the tools, events, and other sources do the selling for him.

> **Homerun!**
> #1.3—Choosing to succeed

When his potential recruits saw that his approach required no sales experience, they began to join him one after the other. By the end of his first year, he was short of his goal of a hefty passive income, but he knew exactly how to get where he wanted to go!

These three individual's stories have been repeated thousands of times to varying degrees by everyone who is succeeding in Pre-Paid Legal. Whatever the challenges or obstacles you might face, when you overcome them, you will have found the shortest route to your success.

My advice to you: ***take it and run!***

Steps To Ensure Personal Success
Chapter #1

1. Recognize that success is **90% attitude** and **10% skill**

2. Allow people's comments, positive or negative, to propel you closer to your **dreams**

3. Remember that the way to succeed in Pre-Paid Legal is to keep moving forward

4. **Believe** in yourself, **expect** to succeed, **visualize** yourself succeeding, and **get excited** about Pre-Paid Legal!

5. Regardless what others say, think, or do, **maintain the focus** on your goals and dreams

6. Understand that the shortest route to your success is found in **overcoming any and every obstacle** in your path

---

Secrets of the Top Producers
"The hardest part is in the beginning.
If you'll just hang in there, you will succeed."
-Mike Melia, Atlanta, GA

The shortest route to your success

Chapter #2 reveals:

- How to apply the secrets of the top producers

- Why enthusiasm and commitment are so important

- The value of being coachable

- How to foster an I-will-not-be-denied attitude

"Justice For All"

7 FOUNDATIONAL QUALITIES OF THE TOP PRODUCERS

Late one night, Joel called Bill and Annette Hamilton, two of Pre-Paid Legal's top producers, and said, "I'm ready to get serious now—what do I need to do?" Joel and his wife had been Associates for more than a year, but in that amount of time had only sold 17 Pre-Paid Legal memberships.

Bill replied, "If you are coachable and teachable and willing to do the things that I teach you to do, we can explode your business!"

Joel heartily agreed, so Bill began flying from Dallas to Charlotte, North Carolina and spending 2 weeks at a time driving up and down the back roads of every town within a 3-hour radius. "We went to small business briefings from 1 to 30 people," Bill says, "many nights Joel and I would get back at 2 or 3 o'clock in the morning, but we were passionate about it!" Within a year, membership sales increased from 17 to 1400!

What was it that Joel did correctly to explode his business? Part of the answer was his I-will-not-be-denied attitude combined with the practical results of taking action, but the other part of the answer is the fact that he tapped into the foundational qualities that had already made Bill Hamilton successful.

Those very qualities will propel every new Associate to great heights.

7 foundational qualities of the top producers

The following qualities do not require years and years of practice, nor do they require perfection. *The secret is that you are aware of them AND that you make the effort to apply them as you begin your Pre-Paid Legal business.*

And the more you apply these qualities, the more you will understand them. Eventually you will be able to teach them to others as naturally as you learned them, but that is further down the road. For now, your concern needs to be implanting these qualities into your mind and heart, and then into your actions.

FOUNDATIONAL QUALITY #1
—attitude before skill

A good attitude comes before good skills. Take, for example, the best salesperson you have ever met. I would guess that in addition to being talented, he or she was also kind, helpful, caring, humorous, sensitive, happy, encouraging, and a great listener. Which came first, the great attitude or the skill that moved you to buy?

> "Whether you believe you can or believe you can't, you are probably right."
> -Henry Ford

Attitude always comes first. Without it, that individual you so admire would unmistakably be a different person AND most likely be in another occupation. In Pre-Paid Legal, as is true in life, 90% of success comes from attitude. The technical aspects of the business are secondary and a mere 10%. ***Always remember that!***

"Anyone with the right kind of attitude can do this," says John Hoffman, one of Pre-Paid Legal's top producers. He adds, "My approach to life is that I love life and I believe in everything we do as a company. Because of that, you can't shake me. Headaches are inevitable, but I'm not shaken by them." With that attitude, the skills he has—or does not have—are almost immaterial!

Dennis Windsor, also a top producer, says that "everyone who succeeds in Pre-Paid Legal is a dreamer." Those same individuals were dreamers BEFORE they ever heard of Pre-Paid Legal.

Any skill you might need can be acquired. It is the attitude that proceeds it that will determine your success. Top producer Alan Erdlee summed it up when he said, "I don't think a new Associate needs anything but an attitude to succeed—the skills come along the way."

FOUNDATIONAL QUALITY #2
—*passionate enthusiasm*

When I sold life insurance, I believed in my product so much that I never met another person who had more life insurance than I did. In my presentation, if the person said, "Well, I

> **Homerun!**
> #2.1—Listening only to the comments of others that encourage you to succeed

already have x-amount of insurance," I would say, "That's nothing, look at this!" Then I would take my insurance policies that I had connected together and flip them open like cascading stairs. My prospective clients were always impressed, simply because I believed 100% in my product.

Such a belief is not only necessary for every Associate in Pre-Paid Legal, it is contagious as well! Your excitement flows out of everything you say and do and it affects how you see people, how you serve them, and how you live your own life.

Steve Melia, one of Pre-Paid Legal's top producers, takes it one step further. "I continually sell myself on the concept," he says, as if knowing the value and benefit of the service isn't enough. Steve understands that passionate enthusiasm attracts people, overcomes objections, and is virtually impenetrable to distractions.

I know many of Pre-Paid Legal's top producers and can say that they are some of the most enthusiastic individuals I have ever met! You are joining a great team!

FOUNDATIONAL QUALITY #3
—serious commitment

Success in Pre-Paid Legal requires commitment, but before you can be committed, you must first take seriously the $249 opportunity you have in front of you. Wouldn't you agree that those who start a $500,000 franchise are dead serious about the work in front of them? That same level of serious commitment is needed, so I suggest that you see your $249 as $249,000 and act accordingly—*your results will be astounding!*

With that mindset, making a serious commitment is only natural. Top producer Kathy Aaron explains, "When I joined Pre-Paid Legal, I knew that

---

Your Name
1234 Main Street
Anytown, Anywhere, 78787
Direct: 202.303.4004 • Fax: 202.303.3003
YOUR LOGIN@prepaidlegal.com • www.prepaidlegal.com/go/YOUR LOGIN

Today's Date

(Your Sponsor's Name)
(Your Sponsor's Address)
(Your Sponsor's City, State, Zip)

Dear (Your Sponsor's Name):

(Body of your letter here.)

I will be here, still actively involved in the process of building my Pre-Paid Legal business, 1 (or 5) year(s) from now.

Over the next 1 (or 5) year(s) I will build my business to the _____ Level.

I will remain coachable, teachable, and willing to learn.

The reason I became involved with Pre-paid Legal is that I want...

I am framing this letter, and will be placing it in my _____ where I can view it daily. To ensure my success, I am also committing publicly by sending additional copies of this letter, all with my original signature, to those listed below.

Sincerely,

(Your Original Signature)

(Your Full Name)

CC: Mr. Harland Stonecipher
       Mr. Wilburn Smith
       (Your Upline Executive Director)
       (Your Upline Platinum Executive Director)

---

if I were starting any other business, a 1-year plan just wouldn't work, so I made a 5-year commitment."

Through thick and thin, she kept herself focused on her goals, letting her commitment keep her in the race. "I've been discouraged and wanted to quit," she admits, "but I chose not to."

What people do when their backs are against the wall will be the deciding factor in their success. A strong commitment is vital. Kathy even told those on her team, "I'll be here in 5 years." That type of commitment brings stability to everyone involved.

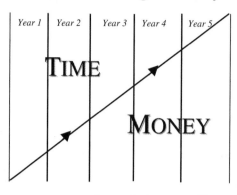

It would be ideal if you set a 5-year commitment, but at minimum, set a 1-year commitment. Top producer Michael Clouse says to every person he recruits, "If you want my time and my personal assistance, then I need a 1-year letter of commitment from you because I need to know you will be here a year from now."

He says this for the benefit of the new Associates. If people will make the commitment, he knows they will perform better and find the success they are seeking much more quickly. Though you may not be asked to make a 1-year or 5-year commitment, those who are succeeding in Pre-Paid Legal have made such a commitment, so make the commitment yourself—you will be glad you did.

FOUNDATIONAL QUALITY #4
—positive and realistic expectations

The goal for many people is to some day have a 6-figure income. With Pre-Paid Legal's infrastructure and support, this goal that can most certainly come to pass, but it will take time—more up front than at the end (see graphs above).

In search of this goal, it is also important to keep your expectations realistic. Top producer John Hoffman makes it plain, "When people say they want to be making $10,000 a month within six months of becoming an Associate, I break it down for them so they know exactly what to do. Then it's just a matter of them applying themselves."

A person can make $10,000 a month within six months of becoming an Associate, and several already have done this and more, **but the key factor is doing what needs to be done to reach this goal.** That is the beauty of Pre-Paid Legal! Whatever your goal, it is possible to reach it! Sure, it will require hard work, but you have to work hard anyway at whatever you do in life, so why not work hard for something that will truly give you a return on your investment!

Another secret of the top producers is that they have a marathon mentality. They want long-term growth **in addition to** short-term growth. The initial growth curve for every new Associate is such an important time and is like the first lap in the race to success. "A lot of people are sick and tired and want out of their jobs quickly," says Ed Parker, a top producer for many years, "but I don't suggest they leave their bread and butter job until their income in Pre-Paid Legal matches their job's salary."

The reason for the gradual approach is founded in Ed's marathon mentality. He understands the importance of the learning curve and the long-term success that is sure to come. "If new Associates jump too soon," Ed points out, "they have to work out of desperation, and that can easily

---

Secrets of the Top Producers

- ♦ Keep a wining attitude
- ♦ Expand associations with like-minded people (positive)
- ♦ Use the proven system already in place
- ♦ Keep a positive expectancy

-Ed Parker, Flower Mound, TX

---

lead to a pressure that is not conducive to selling the service."

Whatever your expectations, Pre-Paid Legal can exceed them. Unfortunately, most of the voices we hear in every day life are negative and attempts at programming us for failure. What we need to always remember is that we can do and be anything we want, and that is what makes the promise of Pre-Paid Legal so incredible!

> "It is what we think we know already that often prevents us from learning."
> -Claude Bernard

You are with a company that is poised for tremendous growth—the timing, the service, and the potential could not be better! Mix in your hard work and growth is inevitable.

FOUNDATIONAL QUALITY #5 —*being coachable*

"You don't have to be smart to be successful," says top producer Larry Smith, "You just have to be smart enough to get around those who are successful, find out what they are doing, and use that system to get to your own success level." That is what being coachable is all about. And with Pre-Paid Legal, you don't have to reinvent the wheel.

> Secrets of the Top Producers
> "Pre-Paid Legal is incredible, the service is sound, and the system is proven. Any road blocks are the ones you bring with you."
> -Dave Savula, Dawsonville, GA

The company has been around since 1972, which means every approach has already been tried. *Your job as a new Associate is the same as that of the top producers: use the system that is already in*

place and that continues to bring results. It's that simple!

The process of being coachable begins with following directions. Larry adds, "When I became a new Associate, I simply followed the advice of Dave Savula, Pre-Paid Legal's top producer, of two presentations a day and one weekly meeting." The results have been outstanding for Larry!

Honestly, the individual who doesn't know much about sales and network marketing often does better in Pre-Paid Legal than someone who knows "everything" about sales. The advantage is found in the willingness to learn, to be coachable, and to follow a system that has been proven to work.

All you need to succeed in Pre-Paid Legal is to plug into the existing system. But for some reason, as top producer Patrick Shaw points out, "A well intending new Associate will often say, 'I have a great new idea to make this work.' Unfortunately, they don't realize the system is already available, simple, and proven to work. Invariably, new Associates' attempts to reinvent the wheel result in confusion and misplaced energy."

The secret? Jump in with a willingness to learn, to grow, and to change. As you add it all together, you get what top producers John and Elizabeth Gardner call "success compression." What this means is that you can learn from those who are successful in Pre-Paid Legal in 10 months what would have taken you 10 years on your own. As a result, John says from experience, "You end up doing in just a few years what others haven't been able to do in a lifetime."

What practical advice—and what an incredible opportunity! From beginning to end, Pre-Paid Legal provides help and training that will propel you well past your dreams.

FOUNDATIONAL QUALITY #6
—doing what others are not willing to do

You have to be willing to do the things that other people aren't willing to do. When I was young and in the insurance industry, I realized that little things, like coming to work on time, being organized, and taking short lunch breaks had a direct relationship to my sales results. In one particular job, I was hired by the company's best salesman and quickly found that he cut corners, wasted time, and was not as focused as he could have been. My goal was to become the top salesman in the company. To get there, I chose to do what he would not do. It sounds simplistic, but I was the top salesman within a month and never relinquished that position until I left the company.

Doing what others are not willing to do can be summed up on 4 words: **turning obstacles into opportunities.**

On a practical level, this will mean:

A)   whatever the obstacle in your way, you find a way around it, over it, or through it

B)   find a way to take advantage of what you have learned or experienced

"The biggest threat that new Associates face is fear," says top producer Alan Erdlee, "but they need to realize that their fear is only something they have created in their own minds." Alan is right, and every fear that is overcome will make that person even

7 foundational qualities of the top producers

stronger. For example, when the fear of being rejected is overcome, it can become a boldness and self-confidence that will not be denied. Any and all fears can be overcome, and those who do so are sure to find success.

Practically speaking, one of the best ways to overcome an obstacle is to have your sponsor or someone else in Pre-Paid Legal help you through it. From talking on the phone to making a presentation, whatever it might be, you are surrounded with a team of people who want to see you succeed. They have also been down the same road and they know how to turn an obstacle into an opportunity.

If you will do what others are not willing to do, your success is imminent.

FOUNDATIONAL QUALITY #7
—an I-will-not-be-denied attitude

I once asked a 42-year-old businessman who owned half a dozen companies, doing half a billion dollars in business each year, what the key factor was in his success.

> Secrets of the Top Producers
> "If a person is coachable, they can learn how to do this business. They do not need to have any special talents beyond that."
> -Larry Smith, Parker, CO

"It is my ability to bounce back from failure, to overcome obstacles, and to take calculated risks," he replied. "I waste no time in worry, doubt, frustration, or even wondering why I face obstacles. I assume I will face obstacles and am not surprised when I do."

What a perfect mentality for Associates in Pre-Paid Legal!

This I-will-not-be-denied attitude won't let your past experiences get you down, much less inhibit future growth. I once had a particularly unsuccessful sales presentation and somehow managed to infuriate the man I was speaking with so much that he walked me to the door to throw me out! I stepped outside, turned around, knocked on the door, and peeked in and said, "Can I try again and pretend we haven't talked yet?"

He didn't laugh and I didn't make a sale, but at least I was ready with a cheerful attitude for my next interview. When you are blind to discouragement, deaf to the suggestion of defeat, and numb to criticism, you are well on your way to a successful career in Pre-Paid Legal.

This is all about being persistent and mentally tough, which, according to top producer Steve Melia, "is more important than any given skill." Persistence and mental toughness never take "no" for an answer.

Like in basketball, an incredible defense will save you from losing, but only a good offense will put points on the board. In Pre-Paid Legal, a commitment to the business is the defense that enables you to stand firm through pressures and challenges, but the offense you need is found in an I-will-not-be-denied attitude.

> **Homerun!**
> #2.2—Knowing what to do and having the persistence to stay with it!

How do you go about forming this persistent and mentally tough attitude? The answer is found in combining the previous Foundational Qualities (attitude, enthusiasm, commitment, positive and realistic expectations, being coachable, doing what others won't do) and adding one last ingredient: **action!**

Action is the pressure that produces diamonds, the power that turns the engine, and the flame that lights the rocket. With action, there are no limitations that cannot be broken! That was precisely what Joel discovered when he asked Bill Hamilton for help. Joel's action connected with Bill's foundational qualities and as a result, Joel's business exploded!

And now that you have the same foundational qualities, let your business explode as well!

Steps To Ensure Personal Success
Chapter #2

1. Pursue the **right attitude** before pursuing the right skill

2. Become **passionate** and **enthusiastic** about Pre-Paid Legal, the service you are providing, and the benefit it is to everyone

3. Complete a **letter of commitment**

4. Have **positive** and **realistic expectations**

5. Be **coachable** and **willing**

6. **Do what others are not willing to do**

7. Set your **I-will-not-be-denied** attitude in motion

> Secrets of the Top Producers
> "If we train someone, it isn't a question as to whether they will be successful or not. They will be successful if they are coachable."
> -Frank AuCoin, Charleston, SC

Chapter #3 reveals:

- What you need to do to get the best start

- The absolute importance of a Game Plan interview

- How to make and prioritize your initial prospect list

- How to formalize your goals

- The Pre-Paid Legal communication system

- What to do during your first week as a new Associate

"Justice For All"

PREPARING FOR A PHENOMENAL START

Mike's goal was to make $20,000 a month. He believed in the opportunity and was 100% excited, but he wisely asked, "What does it take to make $20,000 a month?"

Since he didn't know a thing about network marketing, he called a friend who was very success-ful in another network marketing company and asked for help. His friend said, "The first thing you need to do is sit down and make a list of everybody you know—make a list of at least 200 people." So Mike, the very first night in the business, made a list of 158 people. Then he took that list and priori-tized it, putting the people he knew and who trust-ed him the most at the top of the list.

(One of the most common mistakes that peo-ple make who are new to network marketing and Pre-Paid Legal in particular is that of failing to make a list of at least 100 people. And because they don't make the list, they don't prioritize it either, and therefore fail to call the people on their list.)

With his prioritized list, Mike took the next day off work and began making phone calls. "I made 42 calls," he says, "and received 42 polite 'no thank you' answers." It was a month before Christmas and everyone kept saying, "Sounds like a good idea—call me back in the New Year."

Mike admits, "At that moment I was discour-aged. I was pacing around my house asking myself,

'Am I making a mistake? Is this just a bad judgement call I made?' when a little voice in my head said, 'It isn't a matter of whether or not you **can** do this, but it's a matter of whether or not you **will** do this.'"

At that moment Mike made a resolution: "No matter what, I am going to the top!" When he decided that, he says, "All of the sudden I realized that my only job was to decide who was going with me. That simplified everything for me. I never ever gave up that commitment. I was discouraged, disappointed, beat-up, etc., but I never quit."

> **Secrets of the Top Producers**
> "There are natural laws of harvest. You have to pay your dues before you can reap your rewards."
> -Craig Hepner, Newport Beach, CA

Today, Mike Melia is one of the top producers in Pre-Paid Legal. He did indeed reach and surpass his goal, learning much along the way, including the fact that one of the key ingredients to his success is the simple fact that he made his list, prioritized it, and then got to work on it. Though it was not a glamorous beginning, it was nonetheless the starting point for a very successful career.

Your starting point in Pre-Paid Legal is the same as Mike's, but I am confident that your initial response will be far better than his 0 out of 42!

Where to begin

Your sponsor, the individual who presented you with the opportunity of Pre-Paid Legal and/or helped you fill out your Associate application, will also schedule a Game Plan interview with you. At this Game Plan interview, you and your sponsor will sit down together in a quiet setting (i.e. a restaurant or coffee shop) to discuss the steps necessary for a successful start in Pre-Paid Legal. This can also be done over the phone.

Prior to the Game Plan interview, there are several key areas that must be addressed by every new Associate. What this means is that you have work to do!

The "starting checklist" your sponsor gives you when you first sign up to be an Associate will include all or most of the following items—the order is not that important:

1. Set an appointment time with your sponsor for the Game Plan interview within the next 48 to 72 hours
2. Read the *Fast Start to Success* booklet and listen to the corresponding audio tape
3. Make your initial list of 100 to 200 prospects
4. Write down your one to five year goals, especially concerning home, cars, vacations, and time with family
5. Channel your enthusiasm into preparing for your Game Plan interview instead of telling your friends about Pre-Paid Legal

These five items are the foundational basics to starting out right and cannot be overlooked. Make it your goal to have them all completed within 48 hours. That way you are ready for your Game Plan interview.

The following five steps will be covered by your sponsor during your Game Plan interview:

6. Prioritize your list of 100 to 200 names

7. Get plugged into Pre-Paid Legal's communication systems
8. Buy the Pre-Paid Legal *Success Planner*
9. Schedule to attend the next Fast Start Classroom Training in your area
10. Make a 1-year commitment to your success in Pre-Paid Legal

Whether these last five items are required before or after the Game Plan interview, it really makes no difference; **they are requirements for every Associate who wants to maximize his or her start in Pre-Paid Legal.** Some sponsors prefer to walk you through these last five items so that they can answer any questions and give you additional help along the way.

> Secrets of the Top Producers
> "95% of the fail rate in Pre-Paid Legal is due to the lack of accountability. Yes, you are an independent Associate and in business FOR yourself, but not BY yourself."
> -John Hoffman, Knoxville, TN

The next step is to understand each of these 10 items on your checklist.

#1—Set up your Game Plan interview

This is as easy as coordinating your schedule with that of your sponsor. The Game Plan interview will probably take between 2 and 4 hours. Don't try to rush the interview as it is a pivotal moment in your life, career, and future. **Complete your checklist so you will be better prepared to maximize your results from your Game Plan interview!**

Preparing for a phenomenal start

#2—Read the *Fast Start to Success* booklet and listen to the audio tape

Read this booklet carefully and listen to the audio tape at least twice. The basics outlined in this booklet are vital and help prepare you mentally and practically for making your business a reality and a success. The booklet is available from your sponsor, local Pre-Paid Legal meetings, or Pre-Paid Legal's Marketing Services (580-436-7424).

Ideally, your sponsor will go back through the booklet with you, in person or over the phone, high-lighting key points and answering questions you might have. Both of you will fill out the last page, the *Fast Start to Success* Tabletop Training Completion Form, and fax it to the Corporate Office (580-436-7496) as proof of you completing your Tabletop Training.

#3—Make your initial list of 100 to 200 prospects

Write down the names of everyone you know or even think you know. Do not pre-judge anyone. By thinking thoughts like, "My Uncle wouldn't be interested," whether you are right or not, automatically disquali-fies you from tapping

> **Homerun!**
> #3.1—Making a list, priori-tizing the list, and contact-ing those people on the list

into any of your Uncle's friends. Don't limit yourself or any of the people on your list *because you sim-ply don't know who they know!* (You can take their names off the list later.)

A good example of this is Wilburn Smith, the president of Pre-Paid Legal. Many years ago he recruited Dave Roller into the business. Dave in turn recruited Dave Savula, who went on to be the first million-dollar earner in Pre-Paid Legal! Thousands of members and Associates have been positively affected by Dave Savula. It's a good thing that Wilburn didn't prejudge Dave Roller—and that Dave Roller didn't prejudge Dave Savula. You just never know who people know!

In your *Fast Start to Success* booklet, write every name you can think of on the lines provided for this purpose. If you don't have the booklet, grab 10 sheets of paper and begin. The *Fast Start to Success* booklet has numerous memory joggers to help you as you make your list.

Again, if you don't have the booklet, start here: Who do you know as a result of your:

- parents
- spouse
- kids
- in-laws
- uncles and aunts
- friends
- acquaintances
- business associates
- former business contacts

- hobbies
- sports
- neighbors
- children's activities
- civic clubs
- professional associations
- gym
- and where you do business (banks, restaurants, stores, etc.)

Even check your business receipts, your checkbook, your calendar, and whoever has called you to sell you something. You will quickly find that 100, 200, and even 300 names are not that difficult.

To help you keep your names organized so that you can quickly prioritize them when your list is complete, I suggest that you write across the top of the 10 pieces of paper (or the 10 pages in your

Preparing for a phenomenal start

50

Fast Start to Success booklet) the following headings:

1. current and former associate contacts
2. family (spouse, in-laws, relatives, siblings) contacts
3. hobby and sports contacts
4. clubs and organization contacts
5. where I spend money
6. friends and acquaintances
7. neighbors
8. business owners and leaders
9. my children's activities
10. long-distance contacts

Ask your family, friends, and associates to help you fill each page. Make 2, 3, even 4 columns until it's full. If you ask those who are helping you, "Who do you know?" they might only be able to come up with a few names. But when you ask, "Who do you know from tennis . . . from church . . . from school . . . from work?" they will instantly know a lot of people because you have given them a mental frame of reference or "hook" upon which to hang the names.

If these 10 topics don't work for you, pick you own. Continue until you have exhausted every one of these categories. You will be surprised at how many people you know. Just think, ***everyone on your list knows as many people as you do!***

#4—Write down your one to five year goals, especially concerning home, cars, vacations, time with family, and annual income

Your one to five year goals are the "why" behind your efforts, your dreams, and your actions in Pre-Paid Legal. Top producer Kathy Aaron says, with passion and years of first-hand experience, "If your WHY is big enough, the HOW will take care of itself."

Begin by asking yourself, "What is my reason for becoming an Associate in Pre-Paid Legal?" Do you want to make an additional $500-$1000 a month in part-time income to cover your bills? Do you want to give your children a private education? Do you want to leave the corporate rat race? Are you looking for 6-figure full-time employment? Whatever your reason, write it down on paper.

Your goal must also be something you want personally if you ever expect to achieve it. Dream as though money and time are plentiful and unlimited. Write your goals down no matter how silly they sound. Don't

> **Secrets of the Top Producers**
>
> "I would rather work with a new Associate who acts like a sponge—someone who is simply open to a system that has a proven track record—than any experienced salesperson. You have to be open minded to be properly trained."
>
> -Craig Hepner, Newport Beach, CA

listen to voices that say, "I can't do that." **You can do absolutely anything you want!**

As you begin to formalize your goals, ask these questions:

1. Have I crystallized my thinking about it?
2. Do I have a plan and a deadline for its attainment?
3. Do I have a burning desire?
4. Do I have confidence in myself and my ability to succeed?
5. Do I have an iron-willed determination that says I will pay whatever price necessary to get the job done, regardless of circumstance, crit-

icism, or what other people may say, think or do? When you can answer "yes" to these five questions, then ask one more:

6. Is it worth it to me?

Take your time to really think through your goals, because hazy goals will always bring hazy results, indefinite goals will bring indefinite results, and no goals will bring no results.

From these goals your sponsor will help you craft a Plan of Action. This powerful combination of written goals and planned action has revolutionized the lives and futures of more individuals than I could possibly count. It is an amazing process that will incredibly and positively affect your Pre-Paid Legal business.

#5—Channel your enthusiasm into preparing for your Game Plan interview instead of telling your friends about Pre-Paid Legal

You have a business opportunity in front of you that I believe is second to none. The potential is incalculable! During this exciting time, it is important to recognize that you are in a training and preparing mode. The opportunity to make presentations and offer the service and business opportunity to everyone you know—and make money—will come soon. Right now you need to focus on preparing for your Game Plan interview.

Top producers know from experience that trying to sell memberships or recruit people into Pre-Paid Legal before you have gone through the Game Plan interview might do you more harm than good. When you are trained and ready, you will accomplish 100x what you could if you were to start without proper training.

If you are excited and you really want to start now, call your sponsor and ask if you can listen in as he or she talks to potential prospects over the phone. Better yet, ask your sponsor what you can do. You will probably hear, "Be patient. Finish your checklist. Funnel your excitement into getting prepared." That is because your upcoming Game Plan interview is so important.

It isn't that trying to sell a Pre-Paid Legal membership or sponsor someone into the business before your Game Plan interview will prove impossible. It might work, especially if you use one of Pre-Paid Legal's tools, but it is at the Game Plan interview that you craft your Plan of Action, choose your top prospects, plan your approach for making a presentation, determine the method for following up with each person, and much more!

In short: preparation is vital because preparation will get you where you want to go.

#6—Prioritize your list

With the list of names that you have in place, begin to prioritize them according two criteria: 1) in town or out of state/province and 2) people you have the greatest amount of influence with—they trust you the most. (If you are specifically looking to recruit new Associates, add in a third criteria: 3) people who are successful, teachable, ambitious and have a great attitude. These would then be the focus of your efforts).

> **Homerun!**
> #3.2—Initially waiting to talk to people about Pre-Paid Legal until you understand the service and opportunity a little better

The reason for the "in town or out of state/province" differentiation is that those who are local will be contacted in a manner slightly different than those who are long-distance. Also, if your state requires a license, you can only sell memberships to individuals who live in states that do not require a license. When your license does come in the mail, you are then free to sell memberships in the state for which you are licensed. (Please refer to the "States at a Glance" map for additional information; direct all questions about licensing and commissions for US states or Canada provinces to 580-436-7424 or email licensing@pplsi.com or marketingservices@pplsi.com)

With the names of the people you have the most influence with in descending order, choose your Top 20 individuals. Those are the people you will contact first. The reasoning behind choosing a Top 20 is as follows: of your Top 20 (out of at least 100 names), let's say 3 individuals become Associates.

Out of 100, Top 20 = 3 New Associates

Those 3 new Associates in turn have a Top 20, which adds up to 60 top individuals out of 300 contacts. Let's assume these 3 individuals were able to each get 3 new Associates from their Top 20 lists.

Out of 300, Top 60 = 9 New Associates

Not counting yourself, you now have 12 Associates, 240 top individuals, and 1200 names on your lists. Now, considering the fact that each person on your list knows at least 100 people, you are talking about 120,000 people who are "friends of a friend" of someone you know.

12 New Associates, Top 240 = 1,200 contacts X 100 names each = 120,000 "friends of a friend"

That is amazing! At this rate, you will never run out of people to talk to—*and that is the whole point!*

#7—Get plugged into Pre-Paid Legal's communication systems

Pre-Paid Legal has several areas of communication that each Associate needs to utilize. These include:

♦ **www.prepaidlegal.com**
Immediate access to information, reports, events, documents on demand, and more

♦ **Personalized Pre-Paid Legal website**
Your own website with several personal URLs (Internet addresses), email address, Fast Start to Success Tabletop Training for new Associates, online applications, and more (call 800-699-9004, Option 3 for web support)

♦ **Email blasts**
Regular communications from Pre-Paid Legal's corporate office including notices, announcements, and more (to receive the email blasts, send your email address to marketingservices@pplsi.com)

♦ **Televox Voice Response System**
A virtual office provider that provides you with an 800-number, message and document storing, message sending, pre-recorded messages for whoever calls in to listen, and more (to enroll or

for more information, go to www.televox.cc/ppl or call 1-888-871-4951)

♦ **iComm—the Monday night communication show**
A weekly program provided to eService subscribers via webcast in Associate Services at www.prepaidlegal.com. The show features training and testimonials by some of Pre-Paid Legal's top sales Associates

♦ **The *Connection* Magazine**
A monthly magazine with news and updates about Pre-Paid Legal, success stories, listings, testimonials, information on upcoming events, and Associate recognition (call marketing at 580-436-7424 to subscribe)

Pre-Paid Legal has gone to great lengths to keep you connected. As a company, Pre-Paid Legal knows that the more connected you are with others in the business, the better you will perform and the more money you will make. In short, every communication tool increases your chances for success, *so get connected today!*

#8—Buy the Pre-Paid Legal *Success Planner*

The *Success Planner* is specifically designed for the membership and recruiting needs of every Associate. From goal setting to tracking your goals and from daily routines to keeping organized, this *Success Planner* will help channel your efforts and maximize your productivity like no other daytimer-type product.

Admittedly, the planner does you no good until you know what it is you are planning. That is why your sponsor will most likely ask you to bring it to your Game Plan interview because that is where the planning for your success in Pre-Paid Legal begins.

Preparing for a phenomenal start

WHAT TYPES OF SERVICES DOES TELEVOX OFFER?

♦ A personal toll free number, with the capability of holding nine recruiting messages and nine fax-on-demand documents
♦ A mailbox that allows you to receive voice and fax mail from prospects, other associates, your sponsor, and/or the Corporate Office.
♦ The ability to send messages to group lists, your entire organization or to select portions of your organization
♦ A "follow me" service that enables a caller to speak directly to the mailbox owner
♦ Call screening is also provided to screen out unwanted calls
♦ Full internet access to the system
♦ A cardless calling card, allowing you to easily make calls from a payphone or hotel

Instructions on using the system can be found online at www.televox.cc/ppl or by calling customer service at (888) 871-4951.

After you order your *Success Planner* from Video Plus (800-388-3884), listen to the recorded training session (about 50 minutes in length) on how to use the *Success Planner* (918-222-7308). This planner will be the backbone of your Pre-Paid Legal business. Get it, study it, and become a master at using it everyday—because the success you dream of only comes through careful planning and tracking.

#9—Schedule to attend the next Fast Start Classroom Training in your area

This classroom training is a one-day course packed with valuable information taught by leaders in Pre-Paid Legal (Regional Vice Presidents, Area Coordinators, Platinum Executive Directors, and Gold Executive Directors). Your sponsor can assist you in finding the next Fast Start Classroom Training in your area.

Preparing for a phenomenal start

#10—Make a 1-year commitment to your success in Pre-Paid Legal

Success in Pre-Paid Legal comes to those who are committed to the proven system that is already in place. *It is inevitable!* Top producers understand this—from first-hand experience—and want you to find the success you want, deserve, and desire. Some sponsors will not schedule a Game Plan interview with you until you have signed a 1-year letter of commitment.

> **Homerun!**
> #3.3—Doing the starting checklist and then making it to the Game Plan interview

It's your business, your dreams, and your future. There is no price too big to pay for that! In short, make your 1-year commitment to Pre-Paid Legal—then before you sign it, cross out the "1" and put a "5"! That act alone will put you at the top of a very small 1% of new Associates bound for success.

First things first

Statistics show that the first 24 to 48 hours for new Associates in Pre-Paid Legal are vital. Excitement levels are high and people are ready to get started. "The first thing I do when a new Associate commits to getting started is to give them a 'starting checklist,'" says Patrick Shaw, one of Pre-Paid Legal's top producers. "A new Associate wants to know 'Is it easy? Can I do it? Can I make money?' The checklist keeps us from dumping too much information on the new Associate. It keeps the main thing the main thing!" (Patrick's checklist happens to contain 8 of these above-mentioned 10 items.)

If your sponsor had handed you a pile of training manuals, videos, CDs, cassettes, and inches of text, the odds would be virtually nonexistent that you would ever wade through it all. If we are honest with ourselves, all we want to know is:

1. Is it simple?
2. Can I do it?
3. Can I make money?

From that basis, everything builds, including your enthusiasm and desire to take hold of your Pre-Paid Legal opportunity.

Stepping into your Game Plan interview

Just before your Game Plan interview, your sponsor will call to see if you have completed the items on your checklist. Frank and Theresa AuCoin, top producers in Pre-Paid Legal, take this approach:

We'll call them up the day before the Game Plan interview and say, "I know we are scheduled for tomorrow, but did you finish your checklist?" If they say they didn't do something, then we'll say, "Great. Do you think you could get that done by the Game Plan interview tomorrow or should we re-schedule?"

We don't beat them up about it—they've had enough of that—but we are their business partner and friend and will let them know that we have to hold each other accountable and that we're serious about the checklist.

This call marks the end of your preparation and the beginning of a highly effective training process by which you can achieve every one of your dreams! This process is called

Preparing for a phenomenal start

"checkerboard management" and simply entails that when you take a step, your sponsor will take a step as well. When you push forward, stretch out of your comfort zone and do what you may not have ever done before; your sponsor will be right there with you.

From experience, I have found it is impossible to push people toward success, no matter how hard I try or how much potential they have. You can lead them, possibly even hold their hand, but they must get there under their own strength.

That is why the checklist, which only takes a couple hours to complete, is used as an indicator of future performance. It helps your sponsor know how serious you are about your Pre-Paid Legal business.

> 80 to 90% of all training for a new Associate is the very process by which he or she gets started in Pre-Paid Legal.

Frank AuCoin adds, "If new Associates finish their checklist, then we do sit down with them and go through their goals, put together their approach for their initial contacts, etc. If they will go through it with us and follow the plan, their income could potentially be 5 to 10 thousand dollars a month at this time next year. It's really not all that difficult if you go through it."

By choosing to complete the checklist, you have chosen to succeed! And if you finish early, call your sponsor and schedule an earlier Game Plan interview. It's your future we are talking about, and as Mike Melia said, "It isn't a matter of whether or not you **can** do this, but it's a matter of whether or not you **will** do this."

I believe you can do it! Combine your unlimited potential with the proven system of Pre-Paid Legal and you have all the ingredients necessary for phenomenal success!

Success Note
Remember to complete items #1 - #5 before
your Game Plan interview

Steps To Ensure Personal Success
Chapter #3

1. Set up your **Game Plan interview**

2. Read the ***Fast Start to Success* booklet** and listen to the **audio tape**

3. Make your **initial list** of 100 to 200 prospects

4. Write down your **one to five year goals**, espcially concerning home, cars, vacations, time with family, and annual income

5. **Make it a point** not to talk to anyone about Pre-Paid Legal until you know more about the service and opportunity

6. **Prioritize** your list

7. Get plugged into Pre-Paid Legal's **communication systems**

8. Buy the Pre-Paid Legal ***Success Planner***

9. Schedule to attend the next Fast Start **Classroom Training** in your area

10. Make a **1-year commitment** to your success in Pre-Paid Legal

---

Secrets of the Top Producers
"If you make it to the Game Plan interview, it shows that you are serious enough about the business to have done the checklists, listened to tapes, etc."
-Theresa AuCoin, Charleston, SC

Preparing for a phenomenal start

PART II

STARTING SUCCESSFULLY

Because 80 to 90% of all training for new Associates is the very process by which they get started, it is obviously important that you get started right. The Game Plan interview is a vital part of that process because it focuses on what is most important—YOU!

You will have ample opportunity to learn how to make your Pre-Paid Legal business successful, but it is during the Game Plan interview that the focus is on your "why" for being in the business. When your "why" is clearly defined, reaching your dreams is inevitable.

Kevin Rhea, president of L-K Marketing Group

Chapter #4 reveals:

- The value of forming a lasting relationship first

- Why working together as a team works wonders

- The benefits of accountability

- How to sail through the two phases of growth

"Justice For All"

THE GAME PLAN INTERVIEW

Valencia completed her starting checklist ahead of schedule. The making of her initial list of contacts was encouraging—she couldn't believe she knew so many people! A few of her co-workers and family members helped her reach her goal of 100 names. When her sponsor called to see if she was ready for the Game Plan interview scheduled for the next morning, she almost asked if they could meet earlier, but 9 a.m. was probably as early as her sponsor would want to meet. Valencia was more than ready!

As a schoolteacher and single-mother of two teenage children, Valencia had felt two strong emotions for many years: she never felt like she was getting paid what she was worth and she wanted to spend more time with her children. Pre-Paid Legal offered her the chance to meet both of these goals.

When Tom, her sponsor, arrived at the coffee shop, Valencia was already working on her second cup of coffee. She had arrived early to go over her questions, knowing that Tom would take the time to listen to her concerns and answer her ques-tions.

> Secrets of the Top Producers
> "When your focus is on what the new Associate wants out of Pre-Paid Legal, you are forming a relationship for the long haul."
> —Frank and Theresa AuCoin, Charleston SC

She had talked with him on the phone a couple times and met him at a local meeting just a few days before, but already she was comfortable around him. He was relaxed, not pushy, and seemed truly interested in what she cared about, and on top of it, he promised to train her so that she would know what to do and how to do it. As a teacher, she understood the importance of proper training.

After ordering a coffee, Tom pulled out his starting checklist, the same one he had given Valencia, and said, "Congratulations on completing your checklist—you are closer to success in Pre-Paid Legal than most new Associates! But before we discuss any specifics, like what income you want and how to get there, there are a few things that you need to understand:

1st—you are now part of a team that truly wants the best for you. We intend to do everything we can to help you reach your goals as quickly as possible. You are in business *for* your self, but not *by* yourself.

2nd—we are as committed as you are. Whatever your level of desire or availability, we will work with you to maximize your time and effort.

3rd—you have a joined a team that works together, learns together, plans together, and plays together. If you ever need anything from your team, which includes myself, my wife, or any one else on the team, don't hesitate to ask. We work together because we understand the power and importance of a team.

The Game Plan interview

With that, Tom introduced Valencia to a business model she never knew existed, one that is founded on relationship, teamwork, and the accomplishing of her own dreams.

GAME PLAN INTERVIEW CHECKLIST

☐ 1) Set the appointment with your sponsor
☐ 2) Read the *Fast Start to Success* booklet and listen to the audio tape
☐ 3) Make your initial list of 100 prospects
☐ 4) Write down your one to five year goals
☐ 5) Make it a point not to talk to anyone about Pre-Paid Legal just yet
☐ 6) Prioritize your list of 100-200 names
☐ 7) Get on the communication systems for Pre-Paid Legal
☐ 8) Buy the Pre-Paid Legal *Success Planner*
☐ 9) Schedule to attend the next Fast Start Classroom Training in your area
☐ 10) Make a 1-year commitment to your success in Pre-Paid Legal

---

Success foundation #1
—Forming a lasting relationship

The Game Plan interview is the time to orient new Associates on the specifics of Pre-Paid Legal and, as top producer Bill Hamilton says, "it helps me to know who I am working with. We develop a relationship. They share their dreams and I share some of mine. They share about their family and I share about mine. We make a connection—and that is where it starts."

This forming of a relationship in the Game Plan cannot be achieved in a training session. That is because the Game Plan interview, as top producer Kathy Aaron points out, "is a give and receive mode, while training is a receptor mode only. You need to have both relationship and training, but only in the Game Plan setting can you build a relationship."

Pre-Paid Legal is one of the few businesses that truly understands the importance and value of relationships. "This is the fun part of the business," Kathy adds. Most people want to develop a relationship, and when the people with whom you work are genuinely interested in you and your success, you couldn't ask for anything more!

From a business perspective, a relationship like this leads directly to your success. That is why the Game Plan interview is focused on you! Your sponsor wants to know the dreams and goals you have in life—***so that he or she can help you reach them!***

Many people, adults especially, have not allowed themselves to think out of the box, be creative, and dream since their childhood. In effect, they've turned off their dream machine. Traditional businesses don't allow you to dream very much, especially for personal goals. How often are family goals given any support in the corporate world?

Because of this, many people don't have a picture in their mind of what they want to do "when they grow up." The Game Plan interview is designed to draw that out of them, to get them thinking again.

When you begin to imagine again what it would be like to be and do anything you wanted in life, something inside of you changes. What was status quo is no longer as acceptable—you want something more! And with Pre-Paid Legal, you can have it!

Bill Hamilton may say it best when he explains:

Nothing is more gratifying than to see people catch a vision for something and then to see them achieve what they never thought they would achieve in their lives. One couple I know dreamed of moving from an apartment to their own house—and they did! Another wanted a larger home so their children could sleep in their own bedrooms—and now they are enjoying their new home. These are life-changing moments!

To take people through this process of dreaming, setting goals, and then working to make it come to pass is a delight! People who never allowed themselves to think beyond a job have gone to their employer and said, "I've enjoyed working with you and have learned a lot, but I have an opportunity to embark on a business for myself and I'm going to take it, so in essence, I'm firing you."

Can you imagine the change in those individuals' lives! When the "light goes off," the new Associate begins to believe in what was previously considered impossible. That is what the Game Plan interview is all about—igniting these dreams again, then making a practical plan to reach them.

If you come to the Game Plan interview with your dreams and goals already in progress, the

Part II — Starting successfully

The Game Plan interview

interview will be more of a "how are we going to work together?" session, and it is just as effective.

When you are in business with someone who is doing everything he or she can to help you accomplish your goals and dreams, then you are in the right company. Believe it or not, about 80% of the people in

> **Homerun!**
> #4.1—Going through a Game Plan interview, then putting others through the same process

your life, family included, do not want to see you succeed! But the people you are beginning to surround yourself with in Pre-Paid Legal are truly on your side *and on your team!*

As you can see, the Game Plan interview is about much more than crafting a plan to make money. Sure, money is important, but it is not the foundation to a long-term, successful career in Pre-Paid Legal. The foundation you want is based on a relationship, and from there, anything is possible.

Success foundation #2 —Working together as a team

Your success comes from the people who work with you. Teamwork is a natural follow-through of a lasting relationship. In this setting, you want to see each other succeed. In a traditional

> **Your success comes from the people who work with you**

business, sharing ideas undermines job security, but in Pre-Paid Legal, the more you share, the more you get back. Teammates become more like family as you become involved in each other's lives.

In addition, says top producer John Hoffman, "I want new Associates to be comfortable up front that they are part of a team that is very good and that the team will stick with them all the way." This view of being part of a quality team is important, as John points out, "because you cannot go to the Super Bowl without a team."

It takes teamwork for any great accomplishment, and the greater the accomplishment, the greater the size of the team. Consider the hundreds, even thousands, of people who worked to put the first man

> **"Coming together is a beginning, keeping together is progress, but working together is success."**
> *-Henry Ford*

on the moon! Neil Armstrong will forever be remembered for his accomplishment, but it took an incredible team to get him there.

In many respects, your team in Pre-Paid Legal is the very same! Within this teamwork are three very important factors that must be understood:

A) the accountability factor

B) the safety and support factor

C) the initial two-phase growth factor

A) The accountability factor

Top producers understand that to get what you expect, you must be willing to inspect. This simply means that your sponsor is going to pay close attention to you. Why? Because your sponsor wants to see you succeed. That is what accountability is all about.

A lot of people view accountability as invasive, domineering, and even unnecessary. This couldn't be further from the truth! Remember the starting checklist your sponsor gave you before the Game Plan interview? That was just one part of the accountability process and is an absolutely vital part of your success in Pre-Paid Legal. You completed the items on your checklist, you were accountable, and you are closer to accomplishing your dreams as a result. Accountability is 100% to your benefit!

The way Pre-Paid Legal is set up is that you, as the new Associate, are your sponsor's 1$^{st\ level}$ or top level person. What this simply means is that you are part of the core group with whom your sponsor will devote the majority of his or her time. Your position is one that your sponsor takes very seriously.

> Secrets of the Top Producers
> "The overall purpose of the Game Plan interview is to get the right mindset and attitude before you get into action."
> —Kevin Rhea, Waco, TX

As time goes by you will have your own top-level team, so learn as much as you can about the accountability factor from your sponsor by being accountable. You can't go wrong learning to inspect what you expect.

B) The safety and support factor

With teamwork comes safety and support. You are surrounded by like-minded individuals who dream together and who want to build the business together. This is an incredibly safe place to be.

In addition, you are in an environment where success is continually encouraged through small and large events, whether local or national. Every event is a continuation of the support that exists in your team and is intended to benefit you and everyone in your team. The fact is, every time you and another person are together, you are at an event!

Events not only push you closer to success, but they also nurture the very relationships that you are trying to form through your team. That is why you will find top producers at training events, demonstrating their interest in continuing their learning and in building their team.

C) The initial two-phase growth factor

Every person who starts in Pre-Paid Legal will experience the initial two phases of growth. Both are natural and both are good, but a little help from your sponsor will enable you to quickly grow past these two phases and into long-term, extended growth.

The first phase is the Excitement Phase. Most new Associates are excited (some even lose sleep thinking about their future!) about the potential ahead of them in Pre-Paid Legal—and rightly

> **If you had no Game Plan interview**
>
> Not every Associate will have a sponsor who sees the importance of the Game Plan interview. New Associates are expected to learn from tools, events, or trial and error.
>
> 70% of the way a person is brought into the business is the way he or she thinks the business should be done. This is good when the training is done properly.
>
> Denise Patrick, on the other hand, never had a sponsor, but she went on to lead all of Pre-Paid Legal in individual membership sales for two years in a row! Today she is a sponsor that she always wished she had—and her Associates are a privileged bunch!
>
> Her secret: an if-it's-to-be-it's-up-to-me attitude. Become the type of sponsor you wish you had. Practice your first Game Plan interview on yourself, then with your recruits.

so! Imagine being able to reach your dreams, accomplish your goals, and do what you never before dreamed you could do. It is indeed possible and your sponsor will help you outline the practical steps that you can take to reach your goals.

The second phase, though you might not have experienced it yet, is the Self-Doubt Phase. This occurs as a result of people not catching the same vision for Pre-Paid Legal that you have or people not seeing the need for a membership like you do. This rejection can be unnerving and discouraging at first, which is why you are surrounded by a team that is dedicated to your success. Don't let anyone knock you off course!

Top producer Larry Smith takes a great approach to dealing with this growth phase. He tells his new Associates in their Game Plan interview about the two phases so that they will know what to do when they experience it. "It's all part of the learning curve," Larry says. In fact, the sooner you get through this phase, the better!

Larry asks his new Associates, "When you hit the self-doubt phase, how do you want me to handle it with you? Do you want me to sit down with you and review your goals, discuss your plan of action, etc.? You tell me and that is what I'll do."

That is what teamwork is all about! Larry truly cares and is demonstrating the fact that he is on their side and that he will be right there when they need him. This not only prepares the new Associates for this part of the learning curve, but it also gives Larry the opportunity to call them without any pressure and encourage them in the way that they requested. After all, they are on the same team, so working together toward success is what they do best.

Success foundation #3
—Getting down to basics

The fact that you enter the Game Plan interview with your starting checklist already completed places you miles ahead of most other new Associates! Also, being prepared will allow your sponsor to get down to basics much more quickly, thus enabling you to get to work—and to get paid—right away!

Your sponsor will still want to review many of your checklist items. This is to your benefit, so ask any questions you might have. Upon completing your Game Plan interview and reviewing your *Fast Start to Success* booklet, here are three important items you will want to be sure to complete:

♦ **fax in your *Fast Start to Success* Tabletop Training Completion Form**

This form is located in the back of your *Fast Start to Success* booklet and signifies that your sponsor has taken you through the Fast Start to Success Tabletop Training. Be sure to fax this to the Corporate Office at 580-436-7496.

♦ **schedule to attend a Fast Start Classroom Training**

Attending the Fast Start Classroom Training is a requirement to advance through the compensation plan and qualifies you to receive the $100 training bonus once you have completed the Fast Start to Success Tabletop Training with each new Associate and have faxed in their Tabletop Training Completion

Forms to the Corporate Office. Be sure to take your *Fast Start to Success* booklet with you to your Fast Start Classroom Training.

♦ **set a deadline to meet your 30-day Fast Start qualification requirements to receive higher commissions faster**

You'll receive a 3-year advance commission once you sell 3 memberships and recruit 1 Fast Start ($249) Associate within 30 days from the effective date of your Associate Agreement. If you live

> **Homerun!**
> #4.2—Becoming a true part of the team

in a state that requires you to be licensed to market the membership, you have 60 days from the effective date of your Associate Agreement to be issued a license and an additional 30 days from this date to complete your Fast Start requirements. The Corporate Office must receive a copy of your license. All licensing requirements and directions are included in your Fast Start welcome packet. (Call 580-436-7424, email licensing@pplsi.com, or visit www.prepaidlegal.com if you have further questions.)

This is a good place to give your sponsor a copy of your 1-year (or 5-year) commitment letter.

With these completed, it is time to get down to the remaining 3 fundamentals of your Pre-Paid Legal business that will prepare you to take action:

1. **Your goals on paper**
   —discovering your WHY for being in Pre-Paid Legal, setting specific goals

and writing them down, understanding the compensation plan, etc.

2. **Your plan of action**

—making a plan of action, putting your prioritized list of 100 to 200 prospects into use, knowing when and how to use Pre-Paid Legal's tools, etc.

3. **Your final preparations**

—time management, planning success with your success planner, getting connected with Pre-Paid Legal's communication systems, and organizing your paperwork

The following 3 chapters will cover these important fundamentals for your Pre-Paid Legal success in more detail.

NOTE! If you live in a different city than your sponsor, the Game Plan interview is virtually no different—it's done over the phone instead of in person.

Steps To Ensure Personal Success
Chapter #4

1. Complete your **starting checklist**

2. Meet with your sponsor for your **Game Plan interview** in person or on the phone

3. Give your sponsor a copy of your **letter of commitment**

4. **Recognize** that you are in business *for* yourself, but not *by* yourself

5. **Join the team**!

6. Understand the 3 factors of **teamwork**
   1-Accountability
   2-Safety and support
   3-Initial two phases of growth

7. **Commit** to the process of reaching your goals

Secrets of the Top Producers
"The Game Plan interview is key. The team or person who does this best at the very beginning is the person or team that has the most success."
-Mike Melia, Atlanta, GA

Chapter #5 reveals:

- Why a big WHY is so important

- The benefits of putting your goals on paper

- How the compensation plan works for you

- What your next step should be

"Justice For All"

Your Goals on Paper

What Phil and April wanted out of Pre-Paid Legal was obvious, at least to them. Phil was a schoolteacher in Florida and was facing the prospect of not making more than $33,000 a year for at least another 5 years. They had 3 children, 2 of which were already in school, and April was at home with their 2-year-old daughter. Phil desperately wanted to put all of their children in a private school, but the cost of tuition was simply too much. He also didn't want to see April under pressure to return to work, a prospect that she didn't like either.

Stuck between two equally unpleasant options, Phil was considering a night-job when a Pre-Paid Legal Associate made a group presentation to the teachers at his school. The service made complete sense and he needed his Will done anyway. He asked for the Associate's card and called her later. It took 15 minutes watching a Pre-Paid Legal video to know that he had found the answer to his seemingly impossible situation.

As he prepared for his Game Plan interview, his hands were almost shaking with excitement as he wrote down his goal to place each of his children in a private school. "This is my children's future we are talking about," he almost shouted to himself, "and they are going to the best private school in town!"

Then Phil allowed himself to think a little bigger: "And when they finish high school, what about college? Which colleges will they want to go to?" With that thought, Phil realized he was on a mission, a crusade, to provide the best education for his children!

To say that Phil had a big WHY for being in the business would be an understatement. With his WHY firmly planted in his heart and mind, Phil knew that the practical "how-to" parts of the business would take care of themselves.

Having a big WHY

Whatever your reason for being in Pre-Paid Legal, you need to know what it is. One of the main purposes for the Game Plan Interview is to decide what income you want and how to get there, but before you can decide what income level you are aiming for, you need to have a reason for your goal—*and that is your WHY.*

Top producer Steve Fleming says, "If I recruited you today, I would want to know why you were getting into Pre-Paid Legal." He knows that having a big WHY will do more for your business than anything will. He also knows from

> "The person who knows 'how' will always have a job. The person who knows 'why' will always be the boss."
> -*Diane Ravitch*

experience that the greater the WHY, the greater the level of desire, self-motivation, commitment, enthusiasm, and willingness to learn. Each of these is a necessary ingredient for success, but there is one more step to making it come to pass—*you need to write down your goals.*

Your goals on paper

The magic of putting your goals on paper

A survey taken a few years ago revealed that 3% of people have specific written goals and are heading directly toward them. Another 10%, equally as well educated and determined, do just as much thinking about their goals, the only difference is that those in the first group have **written** specific goals while those in the second group merely think about theirs. The people in the first group outperform the people in the second group anywhere from 10-to-1 to 100-to-1, which

> Secrets of the Top Producers
> "Foster the habit of being thankful for roadblocks, obstacles, and adversity. All they do is push you closer to your goals."
> -Paul J. Meyer, Waco, TX

means those in the second group achieve only a fraction of the success enjoyed by the top 3%!

That is the power of a written goal. A written goal keeps you on track, serves as a checkpoint, and protects you from being overwhelmed by outside distractions.

The third group in the survey was comprised of more than 60% of the people—average people. They set their goals for the most part to extremely short-range objectives: the next raise, the next promotion, etc. They are just getting by financially and seldom take time to think outside of their daily routine.

The balance of those surveyed—nearly 30%— had never considered what they wanted out of life. They are dependent, or at least partially dependent, on others for subsistence.

What differentiates those at the top from everyone else is that *the top 3% wrote down their goals.* Some call it a minor detail, but the difference between those at the top and the rest of society is anything but minor!

Goal setting is simply writing down your dreams, crystallizing your thinking, and then developing a plan with a deadline for its attainment. But before you can write down your goals, specifically the ones that relate to Pre-Paid Legal, you have to know what your options are, how much money you can make in the business, and what it will take to get it. You need to understand the compensation plan.

Understanding the compensation plan

When Mark Brown started in Pre-Paid Legal full-time, after selling his printing business of 18 years, his wife became nervous. She wasn't sure if it would work, so she decided that she would get a part-time job to help make ends meet. It would be a 30-hour a week job at a retail store making $7/hour.

Mark said, "Honey, that will probably equal 40 hours of your time, counting driving, getting ready, etc. all for $210."

He had studied Pre-Paid Legal's compensation plan and knew something she didn't. "If you will help me talk to just a few more people each week," he said, "you won't have to work 40 hours a week!"

With today's compensation plan, a brand-new Associate can make more in three membership sales what Mark's wife could make in an entire week's worth of work! She never ended up going back to work—and she will never have to again because Mark went on to be one of Pre-Paid Legal's top pro-

> **Homerun!**
> #5.1—Having a big WHY
> for being in Pre-Paid Legal

ducers, making far more than his original goal of $1000 a week.

Understanding the compensation plan as it relates to you and your goals is vital. After all, you need to know your target before you take aim. Here is a brief breakdown (a complete breakdown is available at prepaidlegal.com or at 580-436-7424) of the different levels within Pre-Paid Legal and the corresponding commissions earned per level for selling a $26 membership:

Levels within Pre-Paid Legal	Commissions per sale
Associate	$75.00
Senior Associate	$100.00
Manager	$125.00
Director	$150.00
Executive Director	$182.50
Bronze	$189.50
Silver	$194.50
Gold	$198.50
Platinum – Platinum 7	$200.50-$203.50

Now that you know how much you can make per membership sale, you need to decide which level you want to reach. Keep in mind that when you advance to the next level, you make a bonus, called a "bonus override advance," on every membership sale in your organization (your organization consists of you and everyone who has joined Pre-Paid Legal through you), whether you make that sale or not!

The following chart outlines what you need to do to reach each level and the bonus you make per level:

Qualifications per level within Pre-Paid Legal for Fast Start Associates	Bonus per sale
Associate—Welcome to Pre-Paid Legal!	$0.00
Senior Associate—Become a Senior Associate by personally recruiting 3 firstline (Associates you personally sponsor) Fast Start Associates and making 3 personal sales <u>OR</u> make 5 personal sales <u>OR</u> you and your organization sell 50 PPL memberships	$25.00
Manager—Achieve Manager status when you have 3 legs (3 different firstline Associates) with a Senior Associate or above in each one and you attend a FSTS Training Course <u>OR</u> you and your organization sell 100 PPL memberships	$25.00
Director—Achieve Director status when you have 3 legs with a Manager or above in each leg OR you personally sell 250 memberships OR you and your organization sell 250 memberships with no more than 200 memberships from 1 leg	$25.00
Executive Director—Reach Executive Director status when you have 3 legs with an active Director and 75 membership sales. You may count personal sales and up to 25 sales per leg containing an active Director OR personally sell 75 memberships each month.	$32.50
Bronze—Reach Bronze status when you are an Executive Director (ED) and have 1 ED leg or 150 personal sales	$7.00
Silver—Reach Silver status when you are an Executive Director and have 2 ED legs or 200 personal sales	$5.00
Gold—Reach Gold status when you are an Executive Director and have 3 ED legs or 250 personal sales	$4.00
Platinum—Reach Platinum status when you are an Executive Director and have 4 ED leg or 300 personal sales	$2.00
Platinum 2 - Platinum 7—Reach Platinum 2 - Platinum 7 status when you are an Executive Director and have 5-10 ED legs	$0.50

And none of these numbers reflect the fact that you are making a residual income that will be paid to you indefinitely! As long as you remain an active Associate and your members keep their Pre-Paid Legal service, you will receive a residual income. The residual income begins in the 4th year because you are being paid a 3-year advance on every sale now (for more information on residual income, call Marketing at 580-436-7424).

What's the next step?

I believe there are 7 questions that you as a new Associate need to answer immediately. They are as follows:

1. What are your top goals that Pre-Paid Legal can help you achieve?

2. What is your WHY or reason for each of these goals?

3. When exactly would you like to see each goal reached?

4. When do you plan to become a Senior Associate?

5. When do you plan to become a Manager?

6. When do you plan to become a Director?

7. When do you plan to become an Executive Director?

Write the answers to these questions in your *Fast Start to Success* booklet and/or on a piece of paper so that your sponsor can discuss them with you. Also, print the questions and answers in large font and post them on your office wall—doing so will help keep your WHY in front of you.

> **Homerun!**
> #5.2—Writing your goals down on paper

The benefits of putting your goals on paper

When your goals are written down, you know where you are going. What's more:

- ◆ You are sure of your goals, direction, and purpose!
- ◆ You are focused!
- ◆ Your thinking has been crystallized!

- ♦ You are sure and confident!
- ♦ You are purpose-driven!
- ♦ You are motivated!
- ♦ You have a checkpoint from which to measure your success!
- ♦ You are excited and passionate—because they are **your** goals!
- ♦ You are not easily swayed, discouraged, or distracted!
- ♦ You have an I-will-not-be-denied attitude!
- ♦ You are taking aim at your target!
- ♦ You can visualize it! (Remember: You can only be what you visualize yourself being, you can do only what you visualize yourself doing, and you can have only what you visualize yourself having.)
- ♦ You are going to accomplish your goals—and then some!

The biggest overall benefit of writing your goals down on paper is that now you are ready to make a specific plan of action to reach your goals. With such a plan in place, you are set to accomplish your wildest dreams!

For under-paid, schoolteacher Phil and his wife April, they knew their WHY, they had their goals, and they understood how to get there. The only thing between them and their dreams was a Plan of Action.

Your goals on paper

Steps To Ensure Personal Success
Chapter #5

1. Allow yourself to **dream**

2. Know your **WHY** for being in Pre-Paid Legal

3. Put your **goals down in writing**

4. Understand how Pre-Paid Legal's **compensation plan** applies to you

5. Write down your answers to these **7 questions**

   ◆ What are your top goals that Pre-Paid Legal can help you achieve?
   ◆ What is your WHY or reason for each of these goals?
   ◆ When exactly would you like to see each goal reached?
   ◆ When do you plan to become a Senior Associate?
   ◆ When do you plan to become a Manager?
   ◆ When do you plan to become a Director?
   ◆ When do you plan to become an Executive Director?

6. Understand the **benefits** of putting your goals on paper

Secrets of the Top Producers
"If your goals are clearly defined, rejection becomes a non-issue."
-John and Elizabeth Gardner, Darlington, SC

Your goals on paper

Chapter #6 reveals:

- How to create your Plan of Action

- Which tools (videos, CDs, etc.) to use and when

- Specific examples of how to use your tools

- How to contact and follow up with your top 20 prospects

"Justice For All"

Your Plan of Action

"Do you see an opportunity?" Joe asked after showing his friend Carl a Pre-Paid Legal video.

Carl, a full-time college student with several more years to go, replied, "Yes, I do! I don't like the minimum wage job I have and being able to work on my own schedule would be real nice right now."

"How much would you need to earn per month, part-time, to make it worth your time?" Joe asked.

Carl replied, "I'd only need about $700 a month, but $1000 a month would be awesome!"

"How many hours per week could you realistically give the business to develop that income level?" Joe asked.

Carl already understood enough of the compensation plan to know how much he could make. He said, "I usually work 25 hours a week at my job. I'll back that down to 15 hours a week so I have time for Pre-Paid Legal. I can commit 10 hours a week right now for sure. As soon as I get the hang of it, I'll drop my other job and do this 25 hours a week!"

> Secrets of the Top Producers
> "If you have a plan of action, then you can conceive how you are going to reach your goals. And what the mind can conceive and believe, it can achieve!"
> -Kathy Aaron, Helena, MT

"And how many months would you be willing to commit to reach your goal of $700 - $1000 a month?" Joe asked.

Carl stated, "I would commit for at least a year."

"Great!" Joe responded. "If I could show you how to develop a $1000 a month income, working about 10 hours per week for the next year, is there anything else you'd need to know before you got started?"

> **Secrets of the Top Producers**
> "Know what you are supposed to do on a daily basis—then do it! That is all you need to do."
> -Denise Patrick, Houston, TX

Without hesitating, Carl said, "Nope, I'm ready to go! Can we start now?"

Putting it into action

While speaking to Carl, Joe was not only practicing a closing approach he had learned from top trainer Eric Worre, but he was also putting his Plan of Action to work. He knew he personally needed to make 2 presentations or exposures (getting Pre-Paid Legal information into people's hands) per day to reach his goal of 40 exposures per month. Of those exposures, Joe was hoping to sell 20 memberships and get 2 new Associates. For the membership sales at the Senior Associate level (he already had made 3 membership sales and recruited one person), he would make $100 for each membership sale, equaling $2000.

Then with the new Associates he would do the Fast Start to Success Tabletop Training—where he sits down and walks the new Associate through the *Fast Start to Success* booklet and faxes/mails in the last page to the corporate office—and make an additional $100 per person. (Any Fast Start Associate can do the Tabletop Training, but only after you take a local or regional Fast Start Classroom Training course are you paid the $100. There is no charge to Associates taking the Fast Start Classroom Training for the first time.)

All told, Joe was planning on making $2,200 per month. That was his plan and he knew what to do in the 16 hours he allotted himself each week. He had a plan of action and was determined to stick with it. In addition, he knew he would begin to make more each month because his new Associates would begin to make sales, which would mean he would be making bonus override advances on each sale that they made.

> **Homerun!**
> #6.1—Making the number of exposures today that you planned to make

Joe was mixing action with his plan, certain that success would come as a result.

8 easy steps to your Plan of Action

Knowing how to create a Plan of Action for membership sales is absolutely necessary. Once such a plan is in place, adding in other components of the business, such as the number of people you plan to recruit, conference calls, weekly events, etc., would require minimal effort. Here are 8 simple steps to crafting a Plan of Action for membership sales:

1st – clarify your goal per month
—*(i.e. make $1000 a month)*

2nd – take your goal and work backward, dividing up the desired income into weeks per month
—*(i.e. $1000/4weeks = $250 per week)*

3rd – calculate how many personal membership sales would be necessary to reach your goal

> —(i.e. at Senior Associate, each member ship sale is $100, so 2.5 sales per week would be necessary to reach your goal)

4th – determine how many exposures would be necessary each week/each day to reach your sales goal

> —(this number depends on many factors such as the prospect's interest, timing, circumstances, your enthusiasm, experience, etc., but if 1 out of 4 become members, you need to make 10 exposures per week to reach your goal (¼ x 10 = 2.5), which equals 2 exposures per day)

5th – choose an approach to reaching each of your prospects

> —(i.e. via a Pre-Paid Legal video or CD-ROM, 3-way calls with your sponsor, a local event, etc.)

6th – decide how you will follow up with each of your prospects

> —(i.e. 3-way call with your sponsor, 2-on-1 meeting with your prospect and sponsor, listen to a second recorded message, etc.)

7th – schedule the time you will devote to reach your goal

> —(i.e. if you have 10 hours each week for your Pre-Paid Legal business, decide when those hours will be: 2 hours every weekday, 10 hours on Monday, 5 hours on Tuesday and Thursday, etc.)

Your Plan of Action

8th – maintain your daily number of exposures

—(You will reach your goals if you keep to your Plan of Action. In fact, 2 exposures a day is an incredible formula for success. If you stop and add it up, that is about 500 exposures per year! Of those, if 20 became new Associates and they in turn reached as many people as you did, that would be more than 10,000 people exposed to Pre-Paid Legal in one year—and it's your business we are talking about!)

The right tools at the right time

The next challenge is knowing which of Pre-Paid Legal's many tools is the right one to use with your Plan of Action. Because Pre-Paid Legal is continually improv-

> **Secrets of the Top Producers**
> "One of the biggest secrets to success in PPL? Following up on the tools you just sent out."
> *-Dave Savula, Dawsonville, GA*

ing and refining its approach, I suggest that you separate (at least in your mind) the tools into two categories:

A—tools for selling memberships

B—tools for recruiting

Then, whatever the name of the CD, video, audio, etc., simply make sure your prospects have the appropriate tools. Most importantly, before you buy any tools, make sure you know what you need and understand what it is you are buying.

You might also be wondering how much you should spend as a new Associate on tools. It depends primarily on the approach you will most often take with your prospects (i.e. watching a video with them in person is much cheaper than mailing 20 videos to your friends in 20 different states). It also depends on the speed at which you want your business to grow, since experience shows that the more tools you have in circulation, the more sales and more recruits you will have.

Whatever your plan, expect to spend about $100 up front on tools. Most of your tools will remain in circulation as you get some of them back from prospects who are not interested at the time, but make sure you always have a sufficient supply of tools on hand! You will of course need to buy more tools on a monthly basis as your business expands. Add in such expenses as website, newsletter, postage, etc, and you are looking at around $20-$100/month. Top producer Tom Wood points out, "Some of the top producers spend $200-$1000 per month on everything from conference calls to marketing tools. This isn't the only reason why they

An average person in an average week:

Activity	Time Spent	Time remaining in week
Sleep	8 hours/day=56 hours/wk	112 hours
Full-time job	8 hours/day=40 hours/wk	72 hours
Commuting	2 hours/day=14 hours/wk	62 hours
Eating	2 hours/day=14 hours/wk	48 hours
Family/fun	2 hours/day=14 hours/wk	34 hours
Miscellaneous	2 hours/day=14 hours/wk	**20 hours**

-Future Choice (1996), by Michael Clouse

are successful, but it is certainly one of the reasons."

It is also important that you do not overextend yourself by buying more tools than your budget will allow or buying a lot of tools that might not be practical for your prospects. Take it slowly. As your sales increase, buy more tools, that way you

Your Plan of Action

are creating a business with momentum that is also cash-positive!

Using tools for your benefit

The tools that go in the mail are not the only tools that you need to take advantage of. Since a tool is simply something that tells the Pre-Paid Legal story without your help, anything that does this is useful and ought to be used as much as possible. One added benefit of using tools is that anyone can do it—no sales experience or training is necessary— and that is precisely what makes it possible for someone you recruit today to start making money tomorrow!

One of your best tools is your sponsor because you can build your business and be trained at the same time. Having your sponsor help you with your first few membership sales and recruiting presentations, whether in person or over the phone, are the best

> **Homerun!**
> #6.2—Knowing what tool to use, where, and when!

ways to learn. Because most of your business will take place outside of your local area, it will pay to be proficient on the phone for recorded messages, 3-way calls, Game Plan interviews, etc.

Another great tool is the local, regional, and national events. It is here than many prospects "see" the big picture and become Associates. Not only do these events provide training, refreshing, and encouragement for Associates, top producer Alan Erdlee says, "Events are probably the most powerful motivator there is in maintaining some-body's focus and attitude and education and envi-ronment for Pre-Paid Legal."

What's more, events also act as a magnet that draws people into the business. Statistics reveal that the larger the event, the higher the number of guests who sign up to become Associates. So what's stopping you from bringing a busload of people?

Not enough can be said about all the great tools at your fingertips. Whatever the tool, if it tells the Pre-Paid Legal story without your help, then you need to use it. From CDs to Private Business Receptions and from conference calls to tours of Pre-Paid Legal's headquarters in Ada, Oklahoma, whatever the tool, use it to your full advantage.

> **The incredible Power-Play System for flawless presentations:**
> 1. plug in a VCR
> 2. push Power
> 3. push Play

Take the time to become proficient with the tools you use. It won't be long before your business begins to multiply and your goals become a reality.

How to contact and follow up with your top 20

The biggest benefit of a Plan of Action is that once you have such a plan, you know exactly what to do. Usually this means starting with your top 20 prospects and deciding: A) your approach to exposing them to Pre-Paid Legal and B) how you will follow up with them. Here are several approaches and follow-ups by Pre-Paid Legal's top producers for your top 20:

♦ **mail them a Pre-Paid Legal video or CD-ROM**, then when you call, you might say, "A package is on its way. It's a project I'm working on and I'd like your help. I'd like you to

Your Plan of Action

review the information for me. I'll get back to you." The person can't say "no" since the video/CD-ROM is on its way. Once they've watched it, say, "What did you like the best?" From there you move into selling the membership or recruiting the individual.

♦ **watch a Pre-Paid Legal video or CD-ROM together,** then ask what they liked the best and follow their lead (membership sale or recruit). Using a video to tell the Pre-Paid Legal story is always better because the video never makes a mistake and anyone can do it.

♦ **bring them to a local, regional, or national event** to hear, see, and understand the big picture of Pre-Paid Legal.

♦ **call them and then together listen to a short recorded message** by using your 3-way phone service. This will pique their interest (then you send them a video, CD, etc. that they will watch) or this will reveal that they are not interested (saving you both time and you money).

♦ **have your sponsor call them on your behalf,** especially if you believe certain ones of your top 20 would be incredible at Pre-Paid Legal and you are afraid that you might "scare them away."

♦ **host a Private Business Reception (PBR)** in your home or local building and invite as many people as you can, then show a Pre-Paid Legal video and/or have your sponsor or someone else make a presentation.

♦ **have them visit your personalized Pre-Paid Legal website** and watch the Pre-Paid Legal video online (no shipping costs or material costs involved!).

Each of these approaches works well, but it is always important to do your best to pre-qualify a person to some degree. For example, mailing a CD-ROM to someone who doesn't have a computer would be fruitless, not to mention costly.

> **Secrets of the Top Producers**
> "Remember that it takes 5 to 7 exposures on average before a person will see what it is you are trying to tell them."
> *-Ken Smith, Vancouver, B.C., Canada*

Patti Ross, top producer from Canada, pre-qualifies her prospects by having them listen to a 4-minute recorded phone conversation about Pre-Paid Legal's service and opportunity. From there she asks what format they would like further information, then mails a brochure, an audio, a video/CD-ROM, or sends them to her website.

With experience, your ability to communicate (primarily directing people to the tools that Pre-Paid Legal provides) will naturally improve, as will your effectiveness. Mike Melia wisely points out, "We obviously don't master everything in the Game Plan interview. It's an on-going process. It's all about mastering the fundamentals and doing the basics over and over again."

Keep your Plan of Action in front of you

All top producers have this one thing in common: they keep their Plan of Action in front of them at all times. They know what to do, they know what works, and they do it. It is really no more difficult than that.

100

By keeping to your Plan of Action, you are lining yourself up with your target and goal. Keep going and you will hit it, guaranteed!

> Secrets of the Top Producers
> **"It all comes down to what you do today."**
> *-Dave Savula, Dawsonville, GA*

Steps To Ensure Personal Success
Chapter #6

1. Clarify your membership **sales** and **recruiting goals** per month

2. **Take your goal** and work backward, dividing up the desired income/recruits into weeks per month

3. **Calculate** how many personal membership sales/recruits would be necessary to reach your goal

4. **Determine how many exposures** would be necessary each week/each day to reach your goal

5. **Choose an approach** to reaching your prospects

6. Decide how you will **follow up** with each of your prospects

7. **Schedule the time** you will devote to reach your goal

8. **Maintain** your daily number of exposures

9. Keep your **Plan of Action** in front of you at all times

> Secrets of the Top Producers
> "With goals and a Plan of Action, you know what you want and how to get there. What else do you need?"
> -Steve Fleming, Jupiter, FL

Chapter #7 reveals:

- What it means to work full-time part-time

- How top producers measure and balance their time

- How to practically plan for your success

- What forms you need to carry at all times

"Justice For All"

YOUR FINAL PREPARATIONS

Cynthia was quick to put her Plan of Action together. She worked in real estate and had about 30% of her time available to work on Pre-Paid Legal. For her, that equaled about 12 hours a week—just less than 2.5 hours a day.

Her goal was to create an asset that would bring her money every month without her having to expend equal time working for it. In real estate, if she wanted to make more money, she worked harder. But then she had less time to do the things she wanted to do with the extra money she earned. *What she really wanted was time and freedom.*

I've known Cynthia for a number of years and not long ago introduced her to Pre-Paid Legal. After she signed up to become a new Associate, I wrote her the following letter:

Dear Cynthia,

You said at lunch on my porch that you had about 30% of your time that was available to do something. I said, "With 30% of your time in Pre-Paid Legal, you would probably make more money during that time percentage-wise than you would from the other 70% of your time."

So what I would like you to commit to is being full-time in Pre-Paid Legal part-time. What I mean is that during that 30% of every day or week, you will be full-time in Pre-Paid Legal.

Cynthia, when you cross this mental bridge, your mindset will change—your physiology will change—your attitude will change—and your activity and results will change.

There was a guy in Miami, Florida who would only sell insurance for me 20% of his time. However, he was full-time in his own mind and he tried to compress a whole day's work every day into that two hours. He made the Million Dollar Roundtable and became more independently wealthy from his part-time job working with me than he did from his full-time job that "put groceries on the table."

> **Secrets of the Top Producers**
> "We get paid in direct proportion to the value we bring to the market place."
> *-Patrick Shaw, Denver, CO*

Will you commit to being full-time 30% of your time for the next 12 months? If you will, I will personally see to it that you get all the help you need in every way, form, or fashion.

Remember, in the real estate business there are no residuals. You start over every month. I'm not knocking the real estate profession because it is a great business and you can make a lot of money, but the truth is again that when you stop, the income stops. If you put in 30% of your time into Pre-Paid Legal at your current age and produce what I believe you are capable of producing from being full-time part-time, in ten years you would probably be able to join my wife and I in a condo in the Cayman Islands—or possibly a boat (if you like boats).

But the main thing is that the checks will keep coming while you do some kind of charitable community service such as working on your project with the kids.

I am sold on you! You are a winner! I believe in you! I ask the question again: "Will you commit to be full-time part-time?"

Cynthia _____

Notice I left a place for your signature. Return a copy of this letter to me.

Your friend, Paul J. Meyer

Full-time part-time

Most Associates in Pre-Paid Legal are part-time, but that does not mean they make a part-time income! My friend in Miami who sold insurance with me was intently focused on working full-time during the 2 hours that he dedicated to the business each day.

He would have a 3-minute egg timer by the phone. If he didn't have an appointment with you or get what he needed in that amount of time, he got off the phone. He measured his time carefully and averaged 2 presentations

Homerun!
    #7.1—Being full-time part-time

a night, 10 a week. The average salesperson had 15 presentations a week, he had 10, but he worked only 10 hours and they worked 50!

He was a passive, non-aggressive person, but in 2 hours he almost outperformed everyone! He also made the Million Dollar Roundtable every year! His secret? *He was full-time when he was part-time!*

Years ago in the middle of a very busy schedule, I made the commitment to write a training course. My commitment was this: If I am alive, every Tuesday and Thursday from 9 p.m. to midnight, I will work on this course. I didn't vary on my commitment at all. I built my whole life around that and would not reschedule for anything, not even a sale. I was full-time in my part-time efforts. It took me 7 years from start to finish for that course, but when I was done, sales took off like a rocket!

Being full-time part-time is all about one thing: managing your time.

Time management—a trademark of champions

Time management is about much more than making time to do what you want to do (you must **make** the time because you won't **find** the time). Making time is a very important step in the right direction, but what you need to be able to do is measure your time. That is because what you can measure, you can manage, and when you can measure your time, you can also manage it.

Top producer Dennis Windsor is a good example. He operates on the 75-15-10 principle for managing his Pre-Paid Legal time and says, "I make it my DMO (Daily Method of Operation) to do the following:

1. **75% of my time is spent recruiting and selling,** which means I am speaking to someone, making a presentation for either the business opportunity or the membership, on the phone in a 3-way call, at a national event, emailing someone, etc.

2. **15% of my time is spent setting the appointment to recruit** and sell, which means I am giving someone my business card, giving someone a CD or video, calling to see if a package arrived in the mail, etc.

3. **10% of my time is spent finding new people to present to,** which means I am talking to everyone I meet (i.e. cleaners, barbers, waitresses, bag-boys, clerks, airline attendants, etc.) and asking for more names from the people who become members or Associates.

This 75-15-10 rule is what I live by now and I try to teach it to everyone I work with."

Dennis can manage his time because he measures it, and because he measures it, he is always on track. This staying on course is the surest way to reach your goals with Pre-Paid Legal.

Did you notice that "doing paperwork" was not on Dennis' list? To best use your time, paperwork needs to be considered a "filler"—something to do when you can't do anything else. That way you are spending the vast majority of your quality time on what brings a return on your investment.

> Secrets of the Top Producers
> "If you work half as hard in Pre-Paid Legal as you do at your regular job, there is no way you can fail."
> -Mark Brown, Weatherford, TX

To measure your time, you admittedly must be organized, and that is precisely what separates the idle dreamers from the actual achievers.

Planning your success

Systematic and continual organization is a powerful force for attracting success, but organization requires planning and effort. Pre-Paid Legal has gone to great lengths to simplify the process

> **When you can track your growth, you are ready to grow.**

by providing 3 very important tools:

1. A communication system specific to Pre-Paid Legal
2. The Pre-Paid Legal *Success Planner*
3. Pre-Paid Legal forms that are easy-to-file and easy-to-use

1—Pre-Paid Legal's communication systems

When I ran an insurance agency many years ago in Florida, we had one hour of training every morning with the entire sales force. I kept my team focused, growing, and continually moving toward their goals. As a result, we were setting records that the industry had never considered possible. It also stirred up jealousy among other insurance companies in the area.

Attitudes and anger boiled to the point where I was summoned before a review board comprised of fellow agents who threatened to revoke my license because, they claimed, I was strong-arming clients to drop their insurance and buy my insurance. The fact was that when a person already had insurance, I simply sold my policy on top of what they had. I wasn't stealing anything from anyone—I didn't need to.

When they finally gave me a chance to defend myself, I knew I needed to turn the tide quickly, so

I brazenly said, "Who is the best insurance sales-man you have ever met?"

They didn't answer so I started calling people by name and asking them the same question. One after another quietly said, "You are."

"If I am the best salesman, then why in the world would I ever need to stoop so low as to cheat and strong-arm people into canceling their perfectly good insurance for my insurance?"

They didn't have an answer and they did decide to let me keep my license, but what was most interesting was that more than 30 of the men who were in the room that day quit their insurance jobs and came to work for me! I believe it was because they wanted what our team had: excitement, train-ing, focus, and communication.

Without constant communication, enthusi-asm and productiveness will fade away. That is why I kept my team as "close to the fire" (connected, trained, and in sync) as possible.

Pre-Paid Legal under-stands well the importance of staying close to the fire and has specifically designed com-

> **Homerun!**
> #7.2-Getting 3-way calling! Using 3-way calling! Mastering 3-way calling!

munication tools to keep you and your growing team connected, trained, and in sync. Here are 4 such tools that every Associate needs to utilize to the fullest degree:

1. **Your personalized Pre-Paid Legal website**

   Your own website with membership and Associate applications online, complete descriptions of the company, the product, and the opportunity, several personal URLs (Internet addresses), Fast Start to Success

Tabletop Training for new Associates, email address, and more. When you get the service, sign up to receive daily or weekly email blasts that include Pre-Paid Legal's corporate office including notices, announcements, and more (Pre-Paid Legal website support: 1-800-699-9004, option 3)

2. **Televox Voice Response System**

   A virtual office provider that provides you with an 800-number, message and document storing, message sending, pre-recorded messages for whoever calls in to listen, and more (www.televox.cc/ppl or 1-888-871-4951)

3. **The *Connection* Magazine**

   Monthly magazine with news and updates about Pre-Paid Legal, success stories, listings, testimonials, information on upcoming events, and Associate recognition (Marketing: 580-436-7424)

4. **3-way calling**

   Call your local phone company to get this most important communication tool

> **3-WAY CALLING:**
> Order 3-way calling from your local phone company (hookup fee $10±, unlimited monthly service $5±).
>
> **HOW IT WORKS:**
> You call one person, then push the Flash button and call the second person, then push the Flash button again and you are all three on the line at once.

so that you can connect your prospects with your sponsor or a recorded message.

These 4 tools are an absolute must for every Associate. When you stay close to the fire, you are constantly simmering, refining your abilities, and boiling over with contagious enthusiasm! *Get connected and stay connected!*

2—The Pre-Paid Legal *Success Planner*

Behind every top producer's WHY for being in Pre-Paid Legal is a specific Plan of Action that is written down, organized, and followed on a daily basis. To help you build your business, from your Plan of Action to the managing of your recruits, Pre-Paid Legal's *Success Planner* is the tool you need.

Each daily page contains a specific place to write the conference calls for that day, contacts and follow-ups, important action steps, imperative action steps, and your daily accomplishments (see demo daily scheduling page). With your Plan of Action in black and white in front of you, the steps to your success couldn't be any more plain!

A n o t h e r incredible tool that the *Success Planner* provides is the ROMAR (Record Of My Activities Report) system. This is where you track your weekly Plan of Action activities, which immediately reveals whether you are on target to reach your daily and weekly goals or not. Top producer John Hoffman says, "I hold new Associates accountable to their own numbers that they committed to."

The new Associates fax John their completed ROMAR forms once a week. "You are right on target! Keep it up!" John might say, or "I notice that you

RECORD OF MY ACTIVITIES REPORT - (ROMAR)										Name _____ Week Ending _____

MINIMUM OBJECTIVE FOR THIS WEEK	MY DAILY GOAL	MON	TUES	WED	THURS	FRI	SAT	SUN	TOTAL
CALLS TELEPHONE OR IN PERSON									
CONTACTS MADE									
# 3-WAY CALLS W/UPLINE									
# 3-WAY CALLS W/DOWNLINE									
# APPOINTMENTS/ PRESENTATIONS									
# LITERATURE PACKS MAILED									
# NEW MEMBERSHIPS									
# NEW ASSOCIATES									
# FAST START TRAINING KITS PURCHASED									
# FAST START TRAINING KITS CONDUCTED									
COMMISSIONS EARNED									
# NEW PROSPECTS									
# NEW PROSPECTS AT OPP. MTG.									
HOURS WORKED									

	CUMULATIVE TOTAL BROUGHT FORWARD	THIS WEEK'S TOTAL	NEW TOTAL
Contacts Made			A
# New Memberships Sold			B
# New Associates			C
Fast Start Training Kits Sold			D
Commission Earned			E
EVERY TIME I MAKE A CONTACT, IT'S WORTH $ _____			E + A
EVERY TIME A PROSPECT BUYS A MEMBERSHIP, IT'S WORTH $ _____			E + B
EVERY TIME I ENROLL A NEW ASSOCIATE, IT'S WORTH $ _____			E + C
TOTAL COMMISSION EARNED $ _____			C + D

WEEKLY ACTIVITY CHECKLIST

BUILDING FOR LOCAL OPP. MTG.	☐
HOME OPPORTUNITY MEETING	☐
OPPORTUNITY MEETING ATTENDED/GIVEN	☐
BUILDING FOR REGIONAL EVENT	☐
RECRUITING CALL PARTICIPATED	☐
LEADERSHIP MEETINGS	☐
MONDAY CUMMUNICATION SHOW	☐
BUILDING FOR NATIONAL EVENT	☐

haven't made the number of exposures that you planned on making to reach your goal. Is something happening that I can help you with?"

With honesty and compassion, John says, "If I can't inspect their business, I can't expect them to go anywhere. This would be like the CEO who doesn't get the numbers for the entire business—he doesn't know if the business is sinking or floating."

Associates who want to be inspected recognize that the inspection process will only push them closer to their goals. They may not want to fax you their forms if they haven't kept on schedule, but that is when you take them back to their dreams. "How serious were you about wanting to get your kids into a private school?" you might ask, or "How serious were you about getting that new home?"

If they are serious, then they will get back on track as quickly as possible. They are your team members who will go the distance with you. If they aren't serious, then you need to let them know that you will be there to help them when they need it—then you move on. John, like all of Pre-Paid Legal's top producers, would go to great lengths to help someone who is serious about the business, but he leaves the choice in that person's court when he sensibly states, "I would rather have you be wealthy and respect me than love me and be poor."

Directly related to your daily activities is a Personal Profile page that helps you track the training or exposures of every person who becomes a new Associate or buys a membership from you. Keeping track of the most valuable commodity you have in Pre-Paid Legal—*other people*—will help in building a team that is communicating and committed to each other.

The *Success Planner* also provides you with pages for goal planning, contact managing,

PERSONAL PROFILE					
□ ASSOCIATE	□ MEMBER		START DATE		
NAME		SPOUSE			
COMPANY		BUSINESS			
W. ADDRESS		HOME			
		CELL			
H. ADDRESS					
		FRIEND / REFERRAL			
□ FSTS TRAINING ORDERED	□ FSTS TRAINING COMPLETED	□ ASSOCIATE WEBSITE ACTIVATED	□ SALES AIDS ORDERED	□ PPL SUCCESS PLANNER ORDERED	□ GOALS
DATE	DATE	DATE	DATE	DATE	DATE
□ LIST OF CONTACTS	□ THREE-WAY CALLING	□ BUSINESS BRIEFING	□ NATIONAL EVENT	□ FSTS QUALIFIED	□
DATE	DATE	DATE	DATE	DATE	
CONTACT DATE	RESPONSE				FOLLOW-UP

goal tracking, communication planning, itemizing business expenses, and much more. Practically speaking, the *Success Planner* becomes more useful as your business grows.

In addition, as top producer Alan Erdlee says, "new Associates learn the *Success Planner* little by little as they focus on their business, but as the business develops, the personal growth will happen as well." If you haven't already noticed, personal growth and development are vital ingredients in the success of Pre-Paid Legal's top producers. The *Success Planner* makes it easy for you to organize, track, measure **and therefore manage** your success in Pre-Paid Legal, your personal development, and every other area of your life. (For more information on the *Success Planner*, contact Video Plus at 1-800-388-3884 or online at: www.ppltools-video-plus.com.)

3—Pre-Paid Legal forms that are easy-to-file and easy-to-use

Pre-Paid Legal has a minimal amount of paperwork. What they do have has been streamlined so that new Associates can get started as quickly as possible. Here is the short list of items that a new Associate needs when speaking with a prospect:

1. Membership application
2. New Associate application
3. Presentation tool (Pre-Paid Legal flipchart, video, CD, etc.)
4. A CD or Video that can be taken home if the prospect wants more information on Pre-Paid Legal

5. Starting checklist and *Fast Start to Success* booklet with audio to complete prior to a Game Plan interview if prospect becomes an Associate

This information needs to be kept organized and in files wherever your office is located. Remember that both the membership application and the new Associate application are available on your personalized Pre-Paid Legal website.

Always keep a quantity of these items in your car, purse, briefcase, etc. Nothing is worse than saying, "Sorry I don't have anything with me...."

Instead, be prepared and take "missed opportunity" out of your vocabulary.

> **READY BUT WAITING FOR YOUR LICENSE?**
>
> If you live in a state that requires a license to sell Pre-Paid Legal memberships, you can still (while you are waiting for your license to arrive in the mail):
>
> 1. sell memberships in other states that do not require a license
> 2. recruit in your state (they can buy their membership when your license arrives)

Time to take action

After going through the Game Plan interview, creating your list of 100 to 200 prospects, writing down your goals, forming your Plan of Action, familiarizing yourself with the tools, and getting organized, you are no doubt ready to take action.

Top producer Kathy Aaron says every Associate needs to move from WHY to GOAL to HOW to ACTION, and you have done just that!

Your final preparations

You have clearly defined your WHY.
You have your GOALS set out in front of you.
You know HOW to achieve those dreams.

NOW IT IS TIME TO TAKE ACTION!

Steps **T**o **E**nsure **P**ersonal **S**uccess
Chapter #7

1. Work **full-time part-time**

2. Remain true to your **Plan of Action**

3. **Measure and manage** the time you commit to the business

4. **ASAP**—get your personalized Pre-Paid Legal web site, Televox Voice Response System, *Connection* magazine, and 3-way calling

5. Outline your Plan of Action in your ***Success Planner*** and utilize the tools (i.e. the ROMAR system)

6. **File and organize** your Pre-Paid Legal applications and tools

7. Prepare to **take action!**

Secrets of the Top Producers
"Following your Plan of Action
will require organization; following your organization will be
success."
-Kevin Rhea, Waco, TX

Part III

Taking action
TOWARD YOUR SUCCESS

Though you will always be learning and your training will never end, it is now time to take action. In fact, you learn more by taking action than by preparing for it. The secret is to jump in. Don't hold back! The success you create over the next several weeks will be the story that you tell for many years to come.

You know your "why" and you have your Plan of Action, now it is time to put action to your plan. Whatever the results from your first 10, 20, 50, or 100 calls or contacts, keep going. Consistent action is what keeps success coming. You are ready—go!

Kevin Rhea, president of L-K Marketing Group

Chapter #8 reveals:

- The 4 fundamental elements of your success in Pre-Paid Legal

- How to briefly explain the compensation plan

- Why facts tell and stories tell

- A top producer's foolproof presentation

- The importance of exposures

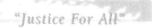

TAKE AIM, TAKE ACTION!

Regina's Plan of Action detailed exactly how she would contact the top 20 from her list of 100 prospects. She had moved to Texas only two months earlier from Oregon, so all of her top 20 prospects lived back home. For her this was handy because Texas requires a license to sell Pre-Paid Legal memberships while Oregon does not, so while she waited for her license to come in the mail, she could start selling memberships to her hometown friends immediately.

Her sponsor, Theresa, held Regina's Game Plan interview over the phone even though they only lived about 20 minutes from each other. Theresa was showing Regina how to build a long-distance business, which was exactly what Regina needed to understand.

With her top 20, Regina decided to mail each of them a Pre-Paid Legal video that showed the need for a membership and the business opportunity. Her first week she would mail out 10 packages and then call to let each person know that a package was in the mail.

> **Secrets of the Top Producers**
> "Focus on the basics and sales will be made and people will be paid."
> -Dennis Windsor, McKinney, TX

"Could you look at the video for me?" Regina would ask each of them when she called. "I'm start-

Take aim, take action

ing work with a New York Stock Exchange company and I'd like your honest opinion." She would then set up a time to call when she was sure they would have had a chance to review the material. The second week she would do the same with the remaining 10 on her list.

In her spare time, Regina ordered some Pre-Paid Legal tools, worked on her presentation script, and listened to training conference calls. It was time to take action, and though Regina was new, she had more than enough to do!

The basics of taking action

Years of training and experience are not required to sell a Pre-Paid Legal membership or recruit someone, but there are several foundational elements of the business that you need to feel comfortable with and be able to explain. They are:

#1—the 5 Titles/benefits of a Pre-Paid Legal membership

#2—the compensation plan

#3—the stories of several Pre-Paid Legal Associates

#4—the different ways to build your business

Yes, using tools is **and will always be** the most effective approach to selling the membership and recruiting others into Pre-Paid Legal, but you still need to master these 4 foundational elements:

Element—#1 The five Titles of a Pre-Paid Legal membership

Knowing what you are selling via videos, CDs, brochures, etc. is absolutely vital. When you understand the 5 Titles, you can explain the benefits with emotion. Here are the 5 Titles of the common $26

Expanded Plan, Legal Shield included, and exclusions that apply per Title:

(Due to regulatory requirements, benefits and rates vary in certain states and provinces. The information contained on this material is for illustrative purposes only and is not a contract. It is intended to provide a general overview of plan coverage; only a plan contract can give actual terms, coverage, amounts, conditions, and exclusions.)

Title I: Preventative Legal Services

♦ Unlimited phone consultation: toll-free access to a provider attorney for personal or business-related legal matters

♦ Phone calls and letters from a provider attorney on a member's behalf on an unlimited number of subjects, including two business letters per year

♦ Contract and document review: an unlimited number of documents, up to 10 pages each, including one business document per year

♦ Standard Will preparation: the member's Will at no added charge with yearly reviews and updates

> **Homerun!**
> #8.1—Being patient along the way, remembering that it takes time to acquire skills, knowledge, and residual income

(Phone Consultation: Nevada residents limited to 50 hours of telephone consultation per year. Letters and Phone Calls: A letter or phone call per subject matter is available if advisable in your Provider Law Firm's sole discretion. Contract and Document Review: Nevada residents limited to 5 personal legal documents reviewed per year. Will Preparation: Trust preparation is available at a 25% discount. A standard Will with yearly updates provided for the primary member at no additional cost. Covered family members can also have their Will prepared for $20 each, with yearly updates for only $20.)

Title II—Motor Vehicle Legal Services

♦ Immediate consultation with a provider attorney upon getting a ticket

♦ Representation for moving traffic violations

♦ Representation for certain motor vehicle-related criminal charges

♦ Up to 2.5 hours for help with driver's license assistance and personal injury/property damage collection assistance of $2,000 or less.

(Motor Vehicle Legal Services: These services are available 15 days after enrollment. Representation under this benefit is provided when the member has a valid driver's license and is driving a properly licensed motor vehicle. Any fines and court costs are the member's expense. Pre-existing conditions, charges of DUI/DWI related matters, drug-related matters, hit-and-run related charges, leaving the scene of an accident, and unmeritorious cases are excluded. Commercial vehicles with more than two axles are not covered. These services are limited to two and one-half (2 1/2) hours of lawyer time per claim and do not include the filing of a lawsuit and exclude personal injury and property claims that exceed $2,000. However, you may receive a 25% discount and consult with your Provider Law Firm under the toll-free consultation benefit for any exclusions under this benefit.)

Title III—Trial Defense Services

♦ If a member of a member's spouse faces a civil suit or job-related criminal charges, the provider attorney will provide up to 75 hours to defend that person at no added cost. Additional pre-trial and trial services are available at a 25% discount off the attorney's standard hourly rate.

♦ The provider attorney will assist the member even if his or her insurance company appoints an attorney.

♦ The longer a membership is kept, the more hours of attorney defense services are included.

(Trial Defense Services: This coverage applies only to the named members and spouse. Divorce, separation, annulment, child custody, or other divorce-related matters, bankruptcy, charges of DUI/DWI, drug-related matters (whether prescribed or not), hit and run, leaving the scene of an accident, and civil or criminal charges occurring as a result of operating a commercial vehicle with more than two axles are not covered under this benefit, but are covered by the preferred member discount. Additional exclusions under this benefit: Being named in a civil lawsuit or having criminal charges filed against you because you are listed as an owner, management, or associate of the business and you had no direct involvement with the act or matter that gave rise to the lawsuit or criminal charge. Those charges are covered with your preferred member discount. If the lawsuit was filed because of something that occurred prior to your membership or because of conditions that were reasonably anticipated or foreseeable prior to your enrollment, then the lawsuit is excluded from your Trial Defense benefit. This exclusion applies even if the lawsuit is filed after you become a member. These lawsuits are covered with your preferred member discount. Class actions, interventions or amicus curiae filings in which the covered member is a party (or potential party) are excluded. Also, this coverage does not include garnishment, attachment, or any other appeal. Your Provider Law Firm has the right to determine whether or not your claim or defense to a matter will prevail in court or is frivolous or without merit. This includes deciding whether or not to appeal any judgement or decision. Your Provider Law Firm also has the right to present your claim or defense according to their independent professional judgement. Pre-Paid Legal will not influence or attempt to modify how your Provider Law firm provides their professional services.)

Title IV—IRS Audit and Legal Services

♦ A total of 50 hours of attorney services, including 1 hour for consultation and advice upon receipt of a written notice from the IRS.

♦ Up to 2.5 hours of consultation and advice after 30 days without settlement.

♦ Up to the balance of 36.5 hours for trial representation

(IRS Audit Legal Services: Does not cover business tax returns, garnishment, attachment or any other appeal, class actions, interventions or amicus curiae filings, charges of tax fraud or income tax evasions, Trust returns, payroll and information returns, partnerships, corporation returns or portions thereof that are included in the member's tax returns, pre-existing conditions—where member has been notified by the IRS prior to enrollment, and services rendered by an enrolled agent. Coverage includes the return due on April 15th of the first membership year.)

Title V—Other Legal Services

♦ The provider attorney will render assistance at a 25% discount off his or her standard hourly rate for legal services not otherwise covered by the membership.

(Preferred Member Discount: Depending on your legal needs, a retainer may be required by your Provider Law Firm prior to services being rendered under this discount. Your Provider Law Firm is responsible for determining the amount of the retainer and any other anticipated costs. Other costs you may incur include fines, court costs, penalties, expert witness fees, bonds, bail bonds, and any out-of-pocket expenses. These costs are your responsibility and are not included as part of membership benefits. Your Provider Law Firm cannot provide any legal services until payment of the retainer and other costs have been made. If you need representation in court, you must notify your Provider Law Firm at least five business days in advance so they may prepare for your case.)

Legal Shield

If you are detained or arrested, call the 24-hour, toll-free Legal Shield number. A Pre-Paid Legal Services representative will then put you in contact with your Provider Law Firm so that you can consult with a lawyer about your detainment. In states where this is available, it only costs $1 a month!

(Legal Shield: The Legal Shield services will not apply if the member is alleged to be under the influence of or impaired by alcohol, intoxicants, controlled substances, chemicals or medicines, whether prescribed or not; the member is alleged to be involved with domestic violence or stalking; the member is being detained for outstanding warrants; the member needs assistance in making, posting, or obtaining bond, bail, or other security required for release.)

Knowing these 5 Titles and the Legal Shield is vitally important, **but being able to explain the value of these benefits is what causes people to want a membership.** For example, "unlimited phone consultation" from Title I is not very descriptive. Top producer Mark Riches has a different approach: "Instead of simply saying 'unlimited phone consultation,' I pick up the phone on the prospect's desk and say, 'This means that you can pick up the phone and call a law firm and discuss any legal matter at any time. You can discuss divorce, credit problems, bankruptcy, taxes, real estate transactions, etc.'"

> **Secrets of the Top Producers**
> "You don't have to sell it; you just need to tell it."
> -Kelvin & Yvetta Collins, Dallas, TX

The fact is that most people will buy a membership based on Title I, so it only makes sense that you describe Title I in a way that is easily understood. Mark points out, "And if you can establish a good value, it is then easy to recruit the person into the business."

Element #2—The compensation plan

The compensation plan has already been described in some detail, but how much should you tell your potential prospects? Top producer Mark Brown says, "I explain the money very simply and up front. I say, 'Here is how you get paid: Pre-Paid Legal knows how much they will pay out for every sale made, they just don't know who is going to get the money yet—you or someone else. At the Associate Level, it's $75 a sale on a $26 a month membership. You get a raise and move to Senior Associate, Manager, or Director through sales or helping other people get into the business, or both. Those you recruit into the business, you get an override on every sale they make, which in most cases is $25 to $75.' That's about all the new prospects need to know."

Or to state it another way: "You make a sale, you get a check, and anyone who makes a sale in your organization, you get a check. It's all paid daily!"

Granted, there are 4 ways to make money in Pre-Paid Legal:

A) personal sales,
B) overrides on sales your organization makes,
C) bonuses for building a big business, and
D) residual income,

but for now, personal sales and overrides are what pertain to new Associates.

Element #3—The stories of several Pre-Paid Legal Associates

Facts tell, stories sell! You must imprint this truth into your heart and mind, then learn 5 to 10 stories of people who have gotten involved in Pre-Paid Legal. Above all, you need to tell your own story, even if you haven't reached the level of success that you are aiming for.

Consider these stories from new Associates:

♦ *"My name is Donny. I've been a teacher for 15 years. I work Pre-Paid Legal part-time, and though this is my first week, I believe in the next year or two I will be making enough to replace the income that took me 15 years to build."*

♦ *"I'm a police officer and all I know is that people need this service."*

♦ *"As a franchise owner, I paid $250,000, but I haven't received half the training that I have in Pre-Paid Legal for only $249 dollars."*

<table>
<tr><td>Homerun!
#8.2—Having the right mindset and attitude before you take action</td></tr>
</table>

These stories are short, but they are also meaningful and motivating. Your story is about why you are in the business—**people can't argue with your WHY!** As you are working on your story, top producer and top trainer Jeff Olson recommends, "Get a tape recorder and tell your story into it. Listen to it for a week and redo it until you like your story. It will change your life!"

Also, and very importantly, use your membership! The more you use it, the more you will believe in it and the greater your story will be. Top producer Denise Patrick said she sold countless memberships by telling her prospects how she used her Pre-Paid Legal membership to right a wrong with her cable company. People could relate, they saw the value, and they bought a membership.

Facts tell, but stories sell!

Element #4—The different ways to build your business

Pre-Paid Legal is a unique company in many respects, but what makes it an even greater opportunity is that you can build your business through direct sales, recruiting, and/or group marketing. It is entirely possible to make a 6-figure income strictly by selling memberships, but recruiting is imperative if you want to leverage your time and expand your business. (Recruiting alone will not bring in the income you need because money is only generated when membership sales are made.)

> Successful people do what unsuccessful people don't do.

From a marketing perspective, you have many different plans to offer your prospects, such as the Standard Plan, Expanded Plan, Law Officers Legal Plan, Commercial Drivers Legal Plan, Foster Parents Legal Plan, Business Owners Legal Solutions Plan, etc. (for more information on these and other specific plans, call 580-436-7424).

With so many plans and the possibility of doing direct sales, recruiting, and/or group marketing, it is important that you begin by narrowing your focus down to one plan and one area of marketing. Then after you gain experience and your confidence increases, branch out.

Does this mean that you should only learn one approach to selling a membership? Of course not! Every Associate should have multiple tools in his or her repertoire, including, as top producer Mark Riches notes: 3-way calling, audio and video tapes, CD-ROMs, conference calls, weekly meetings, and PBRs. Mastering these tools will maximize your effectiveness.

Take aim, take action

Top producer Dave Savula likens this process of learning and succeeding to the making of a superhighway. "Every success road does not start out paved in concrete," he says. "Roads start out as dirt, then gravel, then asphalt, and then the concrete of the superhighways. Experience will take you to the superhighway. Get as much experience as you can so you spend as little time on the dirt and gravel and asphalt as possible."

> **Secrets of the Top Producers**
> "View a presentation as simply an exposure to Pre-Paid Legal—it takes the pressure off of you trying to 'sell' something."
> *-Kevin Rhea, Waco, TX*

Experience, as you know, comes only by taking action.

Making your initial presentation

One of the best presentation approaches that Pre-Paid Legal has used with great success has been Dave Savula's 3-point approach. It is simple and effective. Whichever way you say it, the following 3 points make for an effective presentation:

1. I have something I'd like to show you
2. It will only take 15 minutes
3. You may or may not be interested

The prospects are aware that they have the freedom to choose, which is precisely the atmosphere you want to cultivate. In that relaxed setting, combined with your quality presentation, people will buy a membership from you, thank you for it, and then tell you of their friends who need the same service.

An example of this approach on the telephone might be as follows:

"Hi Bill, this is John. We have never met, but a mutual friend, Carol Steinruck, recommended that I call you. The business I'm with is expanding in your area and she said you knew a lot of people. You may or may not be interested, but if you had 15 minutes to review this material, I'd like to send it to you. Whichever is better, video or CD-ROM, I'll put it in the mail today. Then we can set up a time to talk further. Would that be ok?"

Regardless of the exact words that you use, you need to develop a good membership presentation so that every prospect has a good picture what a Pre-Paid Legal membership covers. If they don't want it at that time, at least they know and understand that it's available. Also, and

> **Secrets of the Top Producers**
> "Spend your first 6 months presenting the service and business opportunity to those on your warm list who: sell you insurance, dry-clean your clothes, cut your hair, etc. Then, with experience and confidence on your side, approach your friends and family."
> *-Steve Fleming, Jupiter, FL*

very importantly, the better the presentation (using tools of course), the more sales you will make!

Be yourself

"Just be normal—that is the formula for success," says top producer Ed Parker. "When you are speaking with people you don't know or haven't spoken with in a while, be friendly. Ask where they are from, how they are doing, etc. If you genuinely are interested and want to be a friend, they will reciprocate."

Take aim, take action

People will buy from friends because there is a level of trust, respect, and consistency that we all want. Truly, every person you befriend is benefiting by your kindness. What's more, friends don't hesitate to give the names of their friends who would also buy a membership or become an Associate.

Very importantly, do not scare your prospects away by using the words "upline, downline, deal, get in to," etc. A lot of people have heard of or experienced what they call "multi-level schemes," and using these words will in their minds classify Pre-Paid Legal as such. Explain that Pre-Paid Legal is a business that sells legal services membership plans, whether through direct sales, group sales, or people you recruit into the business.

Keep it simple, and if you don't know the answers to their questions, say you don't know and that you will find out and get back with them shortly.

Just be yourself, be enthusiastic, and take action!

It's all about exposures

When you introduce someone to Pre-Paid Legal, recognize that it is a series of exposures and not a one-time event. The exposures generally start small and work their way up.

Here is how the conversation between Bill and John might continue:

"Bill, this is John. Thank you for looking at that video I sent you. Do you know several individuals who might be interested?"

Bill might respond: *"Yes, not only do I know some people who might be interested, but I am interested myself."*

John could then say: *"Great! I wasn't sure if you would be or not—I'm glad you are. What I'd like to do is introduce you to Lisa, the person who first showed me this incredible business. Lisa is doing extremely well part-time and works full-time as a tax accountant. Lisa, are you there? Good! Bill, this is Lisa...."*

Near the end of their conversation, Lisa might invite Bill to a local presentation in his area. If John lives relatively close by, she might even say: *"I'm sure John wouldn't mind picking you up for this Tuesday night's meeting."*

From exposure to exposure, Bill is learning more and more about Pre-Paid Legal, which means he understands the service and opportunity much more clearly. And since it takes most people 5 or more exposures to Pre-Paid Legal before they decide to become an Associate, Bill is well on his way.

The approach that you use to expose someone to the business must be duplicable. That way those you recruit into the business already have experience—you used it with them—and can copy what you did. In this case, Bill could be thinking, "I can do what Bill did. He called me, mailed me something, called to discuss it with me, had his sponsor talk to me, and invited me to a local event. How hard is that?"

> **Secrets of the Top Producers**
> "Big success or little success—the difference is in how many people you are willing to expose to Pre-Paid Legal."
> *-Ed Parker, Flower Mound, TX*

Take aim, take action

Exactly! And that is what makes it so easy for new Associates to start making money almost immediately after they sign up!

Top producer Michael Dorsey takes the same approach, only he tries to compress the exposures as much as possible. When he makes a call he introduces himself (and/or explains how he got their name) and with their permission dials them into a 5-minute recorded message that explains a little bit about the company, service, and how to make money. (Using his 3-way phone service, he pushes the Flash button on his phone, then dials the number for the recorded message, then pushes the Flash button again to connect back with the prospect.)

"What did you like best about what you heard?" Michael asks when the recording finishes. He is trying to find what excites them and how interested they are. If they have any interest, he again 3-ways them into a recorded message that is a little longer and a little more detailed. Then he schedules a follow-up phone call. "Are you going to be available next Thursday or Friday? Morning or evening?" he asks, then adds, "The video information package I'm mailing you will have arrived before then."

When he calls to follow up, he checks to see if they have any questions, if they've had a chance to watch the video, and if they've seen his Pre-Paid Legal website. Then he 3-ways them directly to his sponsor or some other 3rd-party expert (people naturally trust a 3rd-party) who will ask questions to determine if they are interested in a membership and/or the opportunity. At this point, the prospect has gone through about 6 exposures. "Most

> **Homerun!**
> #8.3—Spending the vast majority of your time making presentations

prospects are ready to buy a membership or become an Associate at this point," Michael states, "but if they aren't interested, I thank them for their time and move on."

The bottom line goal for every top producer is the same: increase your number of exposures and increase the number of people you expose to Pre-Paid Legal. It's that simple.

Take aim, take action

Steps To Ensure Personal Success
Chapter #8

1. **Understand the 5 Titles** of a Pre-Paid Legal membership so you can demonstrate the value of the service

2. Be able to briefly explain the **compensation plan**

3. Learn **5 to 10 stories** of Associates in Pre-Paid Legal

4. **Practice** your WHY-you-are-in-Pre-Paid Legal story until it encourages, challenges, and motivates *you* to action

5. Internalize this truth: **facts tell, stories sell**

6. **Focus** on one membership plan and one marketing area while your level of experience increases

7. **Master these tools**: 3-way calling, audio and video tapes, CD-ROMs, conference calls, weekly meetings, and PBRs

8. **Always be yourself**

9. **Increase** the number of people you expose to Pre-Paid Legal

> Secrets of the Top Producers
> "I have never seen a 'big deal' work in my life. Thousands have been presented to me, but none of them have worked. A big deal that works is a lot of small deals all strung together."
> -Jeff Olson, Dallas, TX

Chapter #9 reveals:

- Where to start with long-distance prospects

- 5 laws that are linked to your success

- How to become a pro on the telephone

- How top producers recruit long-distance

"Justice For All"

Long-distance Sales and Recruiting

Mr. Mills bought a Pre-Paid Legal membership even though he didn't think he would ever need it. Only a few months later he was involved in a traffic accident where someone died and he was charged with negligible homicide!

He was at retirement age and would have had to sell his condo to cover the legal fees, but because Pre-Paid Legal covers you in the event of a traffic death, whether you are guilty or not, his legal fees were covered—all $30,000 of them!

And very importantly, he was also found not guilty. Today, Mr. Mills still lives in his condo, thanks to Pre-Paid Legal, but one thing has changed—he will never be without his Pre-Paid Legal membership!

Long-distance success—*where to start*

Not everyone will choose Pre-Paid Legal's coverage, but everyone should at least be aware the service exists. To accomplish this massive task, you can either present the information in a face-to-face setting or in a long-distance setting, but since many top producers estimate that at least half of their business is long-distance, you need to become proficient at long-distance sales and recruiting.

What this means is that the telephone will become one of your most valuable and effective tools in building your business.

139

Long-distance sales and recruiting

To maximize your time on the phone, you must first break the force of gravity. Gravity, in this case the reluctance to make a call, fear of rejection, and lack of experience, will weigh you down until you choose to pick up the phone and start dialing. Just as the physical law

> **Secrets of the Top Producers**
> "I'm passionate about the Pre-Paid Legal membership because I know everyone needs it!"
> -Steve Fleming, Jupiter, FL

states that objects in motion tend to stay in motion is true, so it is with making phone calls. The more calls you make, the easier it will be, the better you will become, and the more sales you will have.

To break gravity and to maintain a steady momentum of sales on the phone, there are 5 laws that every new Associate must understand:

#1—The law of averages

Those who have success on the phone are making lots of calls. There is nothing complex about it. That is because the law of averages will always work. If you make 10 calls and sell one membership, you are bound to sell 10 memberships if you make 100 calls, and if you make 1000 calls, you'll sell 100 memberships.

You must also remember that as you get better through practice, your number of sales per call will increase dramatically.

#2—The law of commitment

Whenever top producer Steve Fleming mails a video or CD-ROM to a prospect, he always asks, "Will you promise me that you will watch it by next ____ (day of the week) at ____ (specific time of day) when I call?" Most people will make the promise.

This is a very important part of the process because it puts pressure on the prospects to look at the information, and that is the whole objective.

"When I call the prospects back and they haven't looked at it," Steve points out, "I'll say, 'You promised me' and then pause to let the pressure build. Now they are really pressured to look at it."

He puts them under pressure because he knows they need it more than they think they need it. Consider Mr. Mills!

#3—The law of passion

Passion will cause someone to pause and take a look at Pre-Paid Legal. Passion resonates from your belief in yourself and from your belief that everyone desperately needs this service. It will cause you to say to your prospect, "You owe it to yourself and your family to at least look at the video (CD-ROM, brochure, etc.)."

#4—The law of follow-up

The fortune is in the follow-up. It may take you several calls before your prospects actually look at the material you sent them, but every time you talk to prospects about Pre-Paid Legal, the chances that they will review the information steadily increases.

Following up might be even more profitable than you thought, even if you strike out

100 times. You can always call the prospects back and say, "I know you aren't interested in Pre-Paid Legal, but would you take a look at this video one more time and tell me who you think might be interested in marketing this service?" People will always help you.

> **Homerun!**
> #9.1—Getting rid of the fear of rejection

#5—The law of sowing and reaping

Top producer Craig Hepner says, "The natural laws of harvest suggest that you have to first plant a seed, water it, fertilize it, weed it, etc. before you can harvest it. If you do all the steps properly, you will eventually reap the harvest."

By making phone calls, sending out tools, exposing people to Pre-Paid Legal, following up, etc., it is inevitable that you will reap a harvest of membership sales and recruits. It is inevitable!

Becoming a pro on the telephone

The bottom line is that you need to be good on the phone! Here are several methods, techniques, and skills that I have used over the years to become a master on the telephone:

♦ Set a goal to be the best on the use of the telephone for getting appointments and getting prospects to review your information.

♦ Have a positive attitude toward the use of the phone.

♦ Have all of your prospect lists in the proper sequential order prior to calling.

Long-distance sales and recruiting

- Sit with a mirror in front of you so you can make sure you are smiling while dialing.
- When you are on the phone, visualize seeing the person you are talking with: be friendly, smile friendly, think friendly, and talk friendly.
- Show a genuine interest in the person who is the on the other end of the phone. This is done with the tone of your voice.
- Be honest: "John, I've just gotten involved in a NYSE business. I thought of you. I know we haven't talked in the past 2 years, but I thought you might be interested in this. Is it OK if I send you a video?"
- Be a good listener—a REALLY GOOD LISTENER— of what is said during the phone conversation.
- Stay focused—you have an objective, so stay on track!
- Close on your objective (making appointment or closing a sale), then do the following: hang up and don't keep talking!
- Stand up and take a deep breath, look around, sit down, look in the mirror, and keep on dialing.

With experience your confidence will increase, and with confidence your sales will increase. ***Focus on getting the experience and the sales will follow.***

Recruiting long-distance

You don't have to become the perfect salesperson who knows everything there is to know about the Pre-Paid Legal service and opportunity. ***You simply need to let the tools tell your prospects everything they need to know.***

143

When you do that, you are making room for new Associates who can copy what you are doing. They in turn find success and recommend the Pre-Paid Legal opportunity to people you would normally never have the chance to meet. That is where your business really takes off!

> Secrets of the Top Producers
> "If I'm long-distance, I do not send my prospects to local meetings until they've become Associates."
> -Michael Dorsey, Suwanee, GA

As top producers in Canada, Ken Smith and Patti Ross always say, "It isn't who you know, but who your prospects know and who their prospects know that is going to lead you to your key recruits."

There are numerous ways of doing this long-distance. Here are 5 that are recommended by several of the top producers in Pre-Paid Legal:

Approach #1—using recorded messages

One of the best ways to find new recruits (and sell memberships) is to expose prospects to Pre-Paid Legal through the use of recorded phone messages. They can call the number you give them and listen to a recorded message, but usually you call the prospect and then 3-way into the recorded message yourself.

Since a common objection to talking on the phone is the lack of time, having a 5-minute recorded message is hard to say "no" to. Also, the message is a quality presentation that they cannot interrupt.

If they have no interest, you've only spent 5 minutes of your time and their time and saved money mailing them a video or CD. If they are interested after listening to the recording, you can go on

Long-distance sales and recruiting

to a longer and more detailed message, send them to your website, mail them a video or CD, or invite them to a local event. Top producer Patti Ross says, "Once you have piqued their interest through a recorded message, they are much more likely to follow through to the next exposure."

By using recorded messages, you are answering 2 of the 3 most basic questions that people ask, which are: 1) "Is it simple?" and 2) "Could I do it?" The 3rd question, "Will someone help me?" is an easy one since it is your job and to your benefit to help them.

When someone becomes an Associate, they already know how to sell and recruit—just the way you did with them—and the process continues. Another benefit of using a system-dependent approach is that a presentation by someone who has had no success yet in Pre-Paid Legal is as impressive as a presentation by a top producer. This levels the playing field and gives everyone the chance to succeed.

Approach #2—asking up front questions

Top producer Denise Patrick takes a slightly different approach, but it's equally as effective. She says, "I call people and tell them up front, 'Hi, this is Denise Patrick. I'm with Pre-Paid Legal services. I have no idea whether or not you need to buy this, but this is a sales call. Do you have a few minutes?'"

People are grateful for her honesty, she explains. Then she asks them, "How often do you use an attorney? What do you use them for? Were there times when you didn't use one because it cost too much?"

> ### Subtle script for getting new prospects
>
> "Hi Bob, this is John, I don't know if you've heard, but I recently came on board with an international company out of Oklahoma called Pre-Paid Legal. We are expanding the business in your state and I could use your help. I would like to get you some information on our company that probably isn't for you, but you might know the right type of people we are looking for. Could you help me?"
>
> I didn't ask Bob to buy, sell for me, or join, so there are no barriers. I simply asked for his help.
>
> If he agrees, I send him the information and he takes a good look at Pre-Paid Legal. Whoever he recommends, I call.
>
> *-John Hoffman, Knoxville, TN*

By asking these and other questions, she is trying to show the value of having a member-ship *because she knows that when people understand the value of a mem-bership, they'll buy it!* Telling someone the many reasons why they need a membership is less effective, she has learned from experience, "because people always have excuses for what they don't think they need, but once they see the value, they're sold."

Some prospects seem to have all their bases covered (i.e. their company has a lawyer at their disposal). She then asks, "What would have to happen before you needed to add an external coverage like this?" She usually gets an answer, which is good for the prospects in that it makes them consider their situation.

One individual she called at a business was the actual lawyer the company employed to provide many of the services she was offering. "It was his job I was talking about," she exclaims, "but when I asked what circumstances might change this, he admitted that he was thinking of retiring. He concluded by saying, 'I think the employees here could use something like this.' Had I only told him about why he needed the service, I know he would have said 'no.'"

Asking up front questions enables prospects to see the value behind a Pre-Paid Legal membership, and once they have a membership, what is stopping them from becoming a new Associate themselves and offering the same service to everyone they know? Nothing at all!

Approach #3—inviting to listen to conference calls

Conference calls are valuable tools that can be utilized by numerous prospects at the same time! There are conference calls going on everywhere, whether by Pre-Paid Legal's corporate office or by individual Associates. The conference calls are geared for leadership, new Associates, or for new prospects. Whatever your need, there is probably a conference call within the next few days that will address the issue directly.

Ask your sponsor about the type of conference calls that you want your prospects or Associates to listen to (or call Pre-Paid Legal's marketing services at 580-436-7424 for more information). The conference call may or may not be toll-free, but all you need to do is dial the number, enter a code (if required), and you are automatically connected to the conference call.

To make the conference call more personal with one prospect or Associate, you can call that person, then 3-way into the conference call. You can then hear each other as the recorded or live conference call proceeds.

Approach #4—mail information now, call later

Another effective approach has been to mail a video or CD-ROM to people, then call to say that a package is on the way. The dialogue may vary, but getting your prospects to look at the material is your #1 goal. That is why setting a specific time to call back and discuss it (after the package has arrived) is so necessary.

> **Homerun!**
> #9.2—Learning to connect with your prospect on the phone

When you call back at your predetermined time and ask, "Did you get a chance to review the information?" you will either get a "yes" or a "no." If they haven't, then ask them when they will look at it and schedule a time to call back. If they have watched it and aren't interested, then move to the next exposure.

Top producer Bill Carter takes this approach with his new Associates:

I have new Associates call me, then use their 3-way service and call their prospect. If the prospect has watched the video/CD-ROM, then I am introduced as the Associate's business partner and expert who will answer questions. (I like to be already waiting on the line to make sure I'm available to help. If the prospect hasn't reviewed the information, I immediately hang up.)

With those who have watched the video/CD-ROM, I ask, "What did you like best about what you saw?" The conversation goes on from there in the direction of the prospect's interest: membership or opportunity.

148

My overall job on the 3-way call is to get the person to the next exposure, whether it is a tool, the Associate's website, or a weekly meeting—whatever the Associate wants.

There are multiple benefits to this approach: the prospects experience a quality presentation, a minimal amount of time is spent for everyone involved, sales are made, and the Associate is learning while the sponsor talks. What's more, the new prospect sees how becoming a recruit and making a sale are not all that difficult.

Approach #5—having your sponsor talk to them first

Another approach that is as equally as effective is that of calling prospects directly. Here is what top producer Steve Fleming does in this situation with Amy, a new Associate:

Amy calls someone (Brad in this case) and says, "Brad, I recently went to work for a NYSE company and I've got my business partner on the phone with me, Steve Fleming, and he'd like to tell you a little bit about the service we are selling to see if you are interested. Steve, are you there?"

I then take over and say, "Hey Brad, this is Steve. Amy sure tells me a lot of great things about you. How are you doing?"

I try to create a little conversation, and then say, "We won't take up much of your time, but we work for Pre-Paid Legal Services. It's a legal service company that is very similar to car and health insurance in that it protects people legally. I think you'd agree with me that we live in a very litigious society that

149

Long-distance sales and recruiting

people are constantly being sued and are in need of attorneys for traffic tickets, etc. You really owe it to yourself and your family to take a look at this. Would you take a look at this 15-minute video for Amy?"

If he agrees, then we send it to him (if it's long-distance) or I say, "We'd like to bring it by as it's more effective that way."

If he says, "Can you tell me a little bit more about it?" I say, "I'd like to, but really the video tells you everything about it and we are limited on time tonight, so would you look at the video for Amy?"

Then we go to the next call.

Later, Amy (with Steve on 3-way) will call Brad back to see if he has watched the video (this approach then mirrors #3 above). If Brad isn't interested after he's looked at it, Steve has made it a habit to always ask, "I know you

> **Secrets of the Top Producers**
> "You need high tech (3-way calls, recorded messages, web pages, etc.) and high touch (personal issues, caring, support, friendship, etc.). You need a balance."
> -Michael Dorsey, Suwanee, GA

know the kind of people we are looking for—who are some people we can contact?" Then he and Amy approach whomever Brad recommends.

Steve concludes: "If you will just do this over and over, asking for referrals and calling those on your list, you will be successful in Pre-Paid Legal."

Choosing your approach

Whichever approach you choose, I suggest that you practice it repeatedly until you are proficient at it. Moving from one approach to another will only slow you down and minimize your effectiveness. Maintain your forward momentum by sticking with one approach until you have mastered it, then expand your repertoire.

Long-distance selling and recruiting will prove very beneficial for your business, and every approach you use works just as well in a face-to-face presentation.

Steps To Ensure Personal Success
Chapter #9

1. **Become proficient** at long-distance sales and recruiting

2. **Understand** and **operate** according to:
   ♦ The law of averages
   ♦ The law of commitment
   ♦ The law of passion
   ♦ The law of follow-up

3. **Become a pro on the telephone**
   ♦ Have a positive attitude toward the use of the phone
   ♦ Be prepared every time you call
   ♦ Show interest in the person on the other end of the line
   ♦ Listen—really listen—to your prospect
   ♦ Stay focused
   ♦ Be brief

4. **Choose an approach** to contacting and following up with your prospects

5. **Stick with your approach** until you master it

> **Secrets of the Top Producers**
> "It isn't who you know, but who your prospects know and who their prospects know that is going to lead you to your key recruits."
> *-Ken Smith and Patti Ross,*
> *Vancouver, BC, Canada*

Chapter #10 reveals:

- How to make a face-to-face presentation

- What you need for your first Private Business Reception

- How to make luncheons work for you

- Why corporate events are so powerful

- The best approach for a face-to-face presentation

"Justice For All"

Face-to-face sales and recruiting

"Consider yourself an attorney for a minute," Jesse said as he sat in a restaurant lobby with Phil, a local businessman who happened to ask about the Lady of Justice pin on Jesse's shirt. "How much do attorneys charge per hour? $100 to several hundred dollars, right?"

Phil agreed. In fact, he had a cousin who charged $400 an hour!

"Let's say you're a $100-per-hour attorney," Jesse explained. "What I would like to do is work out a flat monthly fee with you to provide legal services for me, my spouse, and my two teenage children. I'm going to outline some needs I have and as I go through them, I want you to add them up at $100 per hour. Then I want you to tell me how much you would have to charge each month for all these services."

Phil nodded in agreement as Jesse continued.

"First, I would want to be able to pick up the phone and talk with you about any legal matter, personal or business. Of course I will call only during your regular business hours.

"Second, when we need anything of personal legal nature, such as a letter written, a phone call made, or contract reviewed, we would want you to do that for us as well.

"Third, I would like you to draft my Will, then each year review and update it if need be.

Face-to-face sales and recruiting

"Fourth, I want to have this access throughout the United States/Canada. If I'm traveling in another state or province and need legal advice, I expect you to refer me to an attorney in that area. I want that attorney to bill you, and I want you to pay that bill out of this monthly fee arrangement we set up.

> Commit to the process, not the results. The results will always follow.

"Now, if you were my attorney, what flat monthly fee would you charge me for all these services?"

Phil thought for a second, then said, "Probably about $800 a month, but who would pay that much?"

"Somebody might," Jesse said, "but I only pay $26 a month for all this plus a whole lot more!"

Phil leaned forward and said, "Tell me more."

Face-to-face success

When you approach people, you want to approach them in a non-intimidating way. Jesse was simply asking questions and Phil was genuinely interested. There was no strong-arm selling involved.

The "If you've got about 15 minutes, I've got something important I want to show you, you may or may not be interested" approach by top producer Dave Savula has been so effective for this very reason. It is non-intimidating and puts people in an objective mode rather than a defensive mode. And because the product will sell itself, having an objective listener is all you need!

Top producer Larry Smith separates his face-to-face presentations into 3 parts: Approach, Presentation, and Close. To better follow his proven approach, here is how Larry might make a face-to-face presentation:

Approach

If I'm playing golf with several guys I've never met, I'll ask the one I'm with what he does for a living, how long he's lived in the area, etc. He then naturally asks questions about me. I say, "I represent a company called Pre-Paid Legal services." The usual response is, "Pre-Paid Legal—I'm not familiar with that."

Presentation

I say, "Well, let me ask you a couple questions (The #1 rejection to Pre-Paid Legal service is 'I don't need a lawyer,' so I deal with this first): Just out of curiosity, how many times in the last 12 months have you used an attorney?"

Approximately 98% will say they haven't used an attorney, so I then ask, "Out of curiosity, why not?" They usually reply, "I didn't need one."

At this point I use the Feel-Felt-Found theory and say, "I

> **Secrets of the Top Producers**
>
> "Approach people in a non-intimidating open way, ask them questions to let them understand the need for the service, and let them see the business opportunity through the value of the membership."
>
> *-Larry Smith, Parker, CO*

know exactly how you *feel* because that is the way I *felt* when I first looked at Pre-Paid Legal, but when I *found* out the services that Pre-Paid Legal provides and used my 20-20 vision from hindsight, I realized that if I had the service over the years, I would have used attorneys all the time."

They are listening, so I continue. "Let me ask you: have you ever been in the situation where someone was treating you wrong and you knew you were right?" Most likely they will say "Yes, more than once!"

"What did you do?' Usually they did virtually nothing.

"Is there a chance that it will happen again?" Most agree.

"So basically, the first time you did nothing, right? The next time it happens, the way I see it, you really have two choices: do the same thing you did before or you can pick up your phone and call your lawyer and let your lawyer make a phone call or write a letter on your behalf. Which do you think would be more beneficial to you?" They usually smile and quickly agree that the lawyer's help would be most beneficial.

"When was the last time you updated your Will?" I know that 70% of people don't even have one, but asking if it's updated is gentler than asking if they have one.

"When do you need a Will?" The correct answer is always "Right now!"

"Have you ever signed a contract that you were a little unsure of?" They nod their head.

"When you ask a wealthy person to sign a contract, what do they usually do first? They check with their lawyer, correct? Why do they do that and you don't? They can afford it—they practice preventive law while most people sign things and then get in trouble." They often laugh in agreement at this point.

"Have you ever had to make a difficult decision before in your life? Are you smart enough to realize that if you just had legal advice from time to time to find out if you are right or wrong or what your legal rights are, a lot of those difficult decisions would be easier to make?" They keep on agreeing.

"When you think of the word 'lawyer,' what is one of the first words you are forced to think about...money, right? When people are making $10-$30/hr, how much of a lawyer can they afford? Not much!" No disagreement there!

> **Secrets of the Top Producers**
> "Go to the big events because they will cut six months off your learning curve."
> *-Dan Stammen, Plano, TX*

"If attorneys were free, would you be opposed to using them?" The answer is always "No."

"So you aren't opposed to using attorneys, you are just opposed to what . . .paying for them, exactly! And that is precisely what our company does. It removes the intimidation factor by connecting you with the highest quality law firms available in America and you don't have to worry about money. Does that sound like something that makes sense to you?"

Close

Some of the people I've spoken with want the service right then and there, but others say, "It sounds interesting." I then say, "Great, do you have access to a computer or have a working VCR? Why don't you watch this CD-ROM/video (I always have copies in my day planner or briefcase) and see if this service is beneficial to you

Face-to-face sales and recruiting

and your family. Why don't you give me your business card and I'll call you back tomorrow—you can watch this in the next 24 hours, correct? Great, I'll call you back tomorrow to answer any questions you might have."

When I call them back, I just say, "What did you like best about the information you've seen?"

After they answer, I say something to the effect of, "When we talked you said you don't have a Will (or whatever it was they said) and I know that is important to you, correct? Obviously, you also see the other benefits that our service plan offers. In order to activate your first month's membership, it's $26 plus a $10 setup fee, so it's a total financial decision of $36. $36 isn't a major financial decision to you, is it?" They never say it is.

"Ok, how did you want to handle that $36, with a check or credit card?"

I always follow the close by asking for referrals. Then I give them the opportunity to join the business. After years of doing this, I've found that about 90% of the people I make the approach, presentation, and close to will buy the membership and about 20-25% will become Associates. From the referrals, about 15-20% will buy a membership and about 10% will become Associates.

The right tools for face-to-face presentations

You may feel more comfortable with a different approach, presentation, and close, but make sure what you are doing has a proven track record. Following a proven system is the quickest and surest way to reach the level of success you are aiming for.

When it comes to face-to-face presentations to increase your sales and number of recruits, there are other tools that top producers encourage you to utilize. We've mentioned them before, but here are 5 proven tools that will bring results:

#1—Private Business Reception (PBR)

A PBR is the official "grand opening" of your business and should be scheduled as quickly as possible (1-4 weeks) after your Game Plan interview. Many of the people you invite will be interested in the service and/or the opportunity.

Because it is your personal kick-off celebration and because you invite your warm market (people you know, whether casually or closely), top producers recommend that you hold the event in your home. You want the atmosphere to be relaxed and fes-

> **Homerun!**
> #10.1—Enthusiastically showing this product and the opportunity to everybody that you know and that you bump into

tive, but organized enough so that you can make a good presentation to those who come.

The biggest challenge is getting people to your PBR. Here are several tips on getting people there and making the event as profitable as possible:

♦ tell your friends to bring the ice, a drink, etc. (they are then obligated to show up)
♦ don't answer the phone an hour before (people who call to cancel will probably come if they can't get a hold of you)

Face-to-face sales and recruiting

Face-to-face sales and recruiting

- provide a light snack only (a lot of delicious, mouth-watering food will prove to be a distraction)
- be enthusiastic and excited about the value of the service/opportunity you are presenting to your friends
- leave the furniture as you normally have it (if few people come, it's still cozy, if a lot of people come, bringing out more chairs or moving the couch looks good and is perceived positively)
- allow no room for distractions (no children, pets, or telephones)
- start on time and keep it brief (45 minutes)

Usually your sponsor will be there in person to give the presentation and answer questions that people might have, but it works just as well if your sponsor lives in another city. You still play the same presentation video, then instead of having your sponsor speak in person, you introduce, edify, and call your sponsor and let him or her talk over your speakerphone. Those in attendance will undoubtedly have questions, want to see someone who has already been successful in the business, and/or want to hear what you are saying verified by another person, and that is what your sponsor is for.

If your sponsor or another speaker cannot be there or you planned to do the PBR by yourself, that's fine. Keep your approach low-key, personal, and focused on how you have benefited Pre-Paid Legal. For example, you might say, "We finally got our Will done, which brings great peace of mind, and have enjoyed being able to have our lawyers help with documents we need to sign and bills we don't owe. Also, making an extra $500 a month has done wonders for me and my family. I invited you over to show you the same thing. If you are interested, great, it not, that's great too."

Then begin your presentation, which should explain the company, the need in marketplace, the product, the timing, and the compensation plan. Top producers always recommend system-dependent tools, like videos, because a video is flawless in its presentation and easy for new Associates to use. And when the presentation is over, pass out the applications and let people choose what they want to do.

> **Secrets of the Top Producers**
> "Getting people to an executive breakfast or luncheon is easy—who would turn down a free meal?"
> -Eric Worre, Eden Prairie, MN

You might be a little uncomfortable, maybe even scared, about putting on a PBR. Top producer Darnell Self says, "In order to be comfortable, you must first be uncomfortable in the beginning." Good advice! And take it seriously—the more people you invite and the better the PBR, the more sales you will make! Some Associates simply have a PBR once a week and invite new people to hear the presentation, and it works tremendously well!

Also, after doing your own PBR, you will be able to help your future Associates do theirs, and the proven system will continue.

#2—Executive breakfasts/luncheons

An executive breakfast or luncheon is where you buy your guests a meal and show them the Pre-Paid Legal business in a business format. Top trainer Eric Worre says, "Executive breakfasts and luncheons

Face-to-face sales and recruiting

are the single most valuable tool to double and triple your business." The potential is amazing!

How effective are these breakfasts and luncheons? On average, Eric says that out of the 20 business people and 5 to 10 additional guests, approximately 2-3 recruits and 4-5 memberships per presentation will come as a result. (You do the math and calculate how much you will earn at your commission level to gain 3 recruits and 5 memberships each week!)

What does a breakfast or luncheon entail besides your time and the cost of the breakfast or lunch tab? Eric outlines the details:

First, find a restaurant, hotel, or country club that has a meeting room. The room is normally free if you are eating. The food needs to be there immediately at the beginning (buffet or predetermined menu with 2 options, meat or vegetarian). Keep it simple and inexpensive.

Second, promote the breakfast or luncheon. If you are inviting to a Monday breakfast or luncheon, call on Sunday night until you have 10 to 20 confirmed people. 'Let me buy you lunch,' you might say. 'I have something I want to show you.' If you have a few Associates in the area, have them call and get several people to confirm as well.

Third, make the presentation. Exactly when your meal is scheduled to start, stand up and welcome everyone and have them start eating. After 10 to 15 minutes, start the presentation. Use visuals, a video, a guest speaker, or talk yourself. As in a PBR, briefly explain the company, the need in marketplace, the product, the timing, and the compensation plan. You should be able to do it in about 20 minutes.

When the breakfast or luncheon is complete, start preparing for your next one. With your new Associates, start them preparing for their own luncheons. If you aren't exactly sure how you'll do a breakfast or luncheon, what you'll say, etc., Eric concludes, "The best way to get good is by doing it—just start!"

#3—Weekly meetings

Attending weekly meetings is one of the absolute best ways to stay "close to the fire" because it keeps you thinking, planning, and taking action. Hosting the meeting is even better! Another top trainer, Jeff Olson, points out that **if you want more people at your next meeting, rent the hotel room yourself!** You will have more than enough incentive to invite everyone you know. (Everyone at your PBR will also benefit by attending your weekly meetings.)

You could say that weekly meetings are PBRs, except that weekly meetings also function to keep area leaders involved and working together. It fosters a team spirit and friendship level that you don't get at PBRs. You are part of a family! If you aren't in your sponsor's town, those Associates you bring to the business will be your team. Also, if your area doesn't have a weekly meeting or for whatever the reason you want to start your own, then start one yourself.

> **Homerun!**
> #10.2—Taking 2 or 3 things you learn at an event and putting them into practice

Some top producers, like Rodney Sommerville, are selective in who they invite to their weekly meetings. "We invite only people who already qualified to attend the meeting," he says, "and to qualify, they have to previously be in on a 3-way call, attend another event, visit our website, use a tool, or have expressed a genuine interest in the service already." The benefit of this is that the people at the weekly meeting are more focused, more likely to buy a membership, and more interested in becoming Associates.

Weekly meetings will increase your business, so be there yourself and bring along as many friends as you can!

#4—Corporate events

Taking prospects to corporate events will enable them to see the big picture of Pre-Paid Legal, making them even more likely to buy a membership or become an Associate!

Taking your Associates with you will encourage, equip, and excite them as well. Someone said that if you arrive at an event with several prospects and/or Associates, the event is for them, but if you arrive alone, the event is for you. Think about that for a minute!

The bottom line is that events are good for your business. Top producers John and Elizabeth Gardner say, "If you'll just show up at these events, you'll succeed." They know that everyone is equipped and encouraged to succeed simply by attending. "Something special happens at these events that every Associate needs to be a part of," they say. "If you plug in, your business will grow."

Top producer Darnell Self tells of a new Associate who had only been in the business for a few weeks and who went to a training event. She came back and 60 days later she was an Executive Director! She obviously had to put a lot of work into it, but her passion was ignited by going to an event.

Going to the events looks like a big commitment, but the benefits—passion, vision, excitement, knowledge, insight, camaraderie, increased sales, planning, training— far outweigh the costs of time and money. Top Producer Mike Melia tells of a divorced mom who became an Associate

> **Secrets of the Top Producers**
> "It's a serious product, but it isn't a product that requires lawyer's jargon."
> -Denise Patrick, Houston, TX

when she had a 12-year-old son and 9-year-old daughter to take care of. One night a week the kids stayed with their dad while she went to the weekly meeting and he took them to school. One Saturday a month they stayed at their dad's while she went to the monthly training and the same when she went to the annual events. She took the events and meetings seriously because she understood the reward of her attending. Where there is a will, there is a way.

Another factor to consider, says Darnell, "is that people buy a membership because of your excitement and belief in the service." People are also recruited the same way, says fellow top producer, Mark Riches. Events are full of real people telling great stories about the Pre-Paid Legal, the service, and/or how they have benefited from the opportunity. You need to hear it again and again to keep your batteries recharged and those you bring need to hear it so they buy the membership or become an Associate. Either way, you win.

#5—1-on-1 and 2-on-1 presentations

The 1-on-1 presentation is a proven tool known also as the "3-foot rule," which simply means that *everyone within 3 feet of you is a prospect who needs to hear about Pre-Paid Legal.* I like to think that everyone I see not only needs it, but they *want* it!

You need a door opener or conversation starter with someone you don't know, but you can use almost anything, such as the weather, sports, haircut, shoes, etc. Top producer Steve Fleming says,

> A few years ago our family moved to Florida and my wife needed a nail technician. I used her need to start conversations with women I'd meet in stores, banks, restaurants, etc. It was my door opener. Then I would ask, 'Are you from around here? What do you do for a living?' They would then ask me what I did. From there I told them about Pre-Paid Legal, gave them my business card and sent them to my website, and then called them back. We ended up with numerous membership sales and more nail technicians as Associates than my wife would ever need.

There are people everywhere who need a membership or are looking for the opportunity that only Pre-Paid Legal can provide. In fact, they are only an arm's length away from you every day!

With 2-on-1 presentations, your sponsor (or another "expert") is brought in to help explain the service, make a sale, or recruit someone you believe would be an absolute superstar in the business. The benefit of a live 3rd party, rather than validation from a magazine or video, is extremely powerful. When you know a potential superstar, don't hesitate to ask for help. After all, your superstar friend needs what you are offering, he or she just doesn't know it yet.

From a friend to a friend

In every face-to-face opportunity, always ask yourself, "Would I want to be introduced to Pre-Paid Legal the way I am introducing it to this person?" In essence, it's the Golden Rule of doing to others as you want them to do to you, and it works beautifully with your presentations.

I have heard numerous top producers say that they want to make millions of friends. That shows their heart behind their actions, and I have no doubt that they some day will have thousands, maybe even millions of friends.

When someone is a friend, there is no pressure to "sell" anything. Top producer Denise Patrick found that as a member, she would gossip about how good the Pre-Paid Legal service was and how she used it. All her friends starting buying memberships. Then when she became an Associate, she says, "It was as if something 'clicked' in my mind and I started trying to sell my friends on the service. Nobody bought a thing!"

When she went back to her original friendly approach—telling instead of selling—people started buying again. She tells her prospects, like they are her friends, "When you get the service, use it! Get your Will done. Use your attorneys every time you can—make it worth your investment."

When her friends become members, they then tell their friends and they tell their friends, and before you know it, Denise has more friends than she ever imagined.

Those are the types of face-to-face presentations you want to make!

Steps To Ensure Personal Success
Chapter #10

1. Learn the "**If you were my attorney**" story

2. **Remember your goal** in face-to-face presentations is to have your prospect listen to you objectively

3. **Master your approach, presentation, and close**

4. **Schedule your PBR** within 1 to 4 weeks of your Game Plan interview—but you can have as many as you want!

5. Conduct **Executive Breakfasts** and **Luncheons** and encourage your Associates to do the same

6. **Attend weekly meetings** and bring along as many prospects, members, and Associates as you can

7. Use **1-on-1** and **2-on-1** presentations as much as possible—do this on a daily basis

8. Seek to **build friendships** by the thousands!

> Secrets of the Top Producers
> "This business is nothing more than a series of exposures. Keep it simple."
> -KC Townes, Universal City, TX

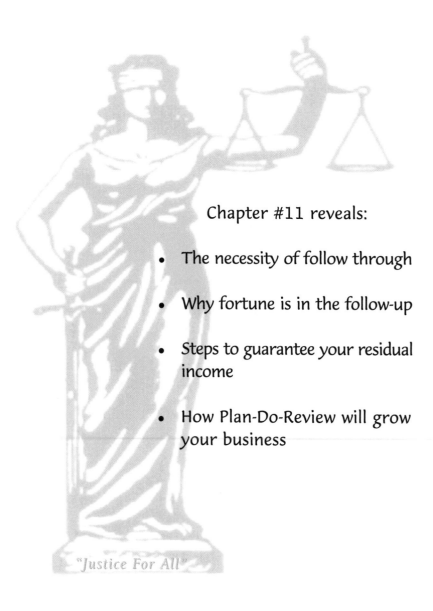

Chapter #11 reveals:

- The necessity of follow through

- Why fortune is in the follow-up

- Steps to guarantee your residual income

- How Plan-Do-Review will grow your business

"Justice For All"

FOLLOW THROUGH TO FOLLOW UP

After 20 years in corporate America, Larry was downsized in January 1996. "I was dead broke, $31,000 in debt, and had to deliver newspapers and sack groceries to put food on the table," he says.

That same month he was introduced to Pre-Paid Legal and began working 10 hours a week. By the 3rd month, Larry was making more than all his full-time work combined, so he quit everything else and went full-time with Pre-Paid Legal. Business grew rapidly and within his first year he was able to pay off his debt, the second year he bought an expensive home in Colorado.

"I made it a point to not just talk to two people but to actually get the information in two people's hands every day," Larry explains, "I planted those seeds on a daily basis. I knew it would start off slow, but as I continued to do the basic things on a daily basis, I knew it would compound over time."

Compound it did—his business exploded! Today, Larry Smith is one of Pre-Paid Legal's top producers.

Secrets of compound growth

What was Larry's secret? Actually, there are two secrets, and they are the same secrets that every other top producer knows:

Secret #1—follow through on your own Plan of Action/commitment to Pre-Paid Legal and follow through with the Associates you help into the business.

Secret #2—follow up with the sales leads and contacts that your Plan of Action/commitment to Pre-Paid Legal brings and follow up with the Associates you help into the business.

> Secrets of the Top Producers
> "You have to practice what you want to get better at."
> -Kathy Aaron, Helena, MT

"Most people follow through," says top producer Dave Savula, "but not that many people follow up." The real secret is this: combining follow-through with follow-up.

The benefits of follow-through

From your Game Plan interview and events you attend to the tools you mail out and your Approach, Presentation, and Close, it is all about following through with your commitment to yourself, your Plan of Action, your team, and your Associates. When you do that, success is just around the corner—if not closer!

One of the primary ways that top producers follow through is in the area of training. They know from experience that inexperienced Associates who are properly trained will outperform superstar salespeople 10 times out of 10. It's a proven fact, which is why top producers stress being teachable and following only what has been proven to work within Pre-Paid Legal.

Top producer Ed Parker says matter-of-factly, "The best trained team always wins." Another top producer, Craig Hepner, is literally fanatical about training. He and those in his organization hold training sessions for more than a thousand people at a time! Craig notes, "A lot of people recognize that Pre-Paid Legal is a rock-solid company, that the product is a common-sense product, and that the compensation plan is very lucrative, but what they want to know is 'Can I do it?' We take the guesswork out of the business."

> **How to open a FedEx account:**
> The only way to overnight membership and Associate applications to Pre-Paid Legal is via FedEx. To open an account (free), order pre-printed labels & envelopes, request pickup, track shipments: phone 800-GO-FEDEX (800-463-3339) or go online at: www.fedex.com (a sample label is available in Documents-on-Demand at www.prepaidlegal.com).
> Be sure the following is on your free pre-printed FedEx airbills:
>
> ♦ your Associate number
> ♦ bill to: recipient
> ♦ account number: 1013-4210-7
>
> Discounted rates for Associates are $7/shipment (up to 3 pounds) and will be charged against your commission account.
> *Your new Associate Fast Start kit contains this FedEx information*

The results of such an emphasis on training are extraordinary. Of those in his team, several have marketed thousands of memberships through their respective organizations! "We even had one gentleman who reached Executive Director level in 14 days!" Craig says, then adds, "and he attributed his success to training."

Between corporate events, Craig's team has weekend events, and between those, weekly events, and between those, conference calls, and between those, email broadcasts. "We are keeping people plugged in, communicating to them, and constantly

Follow through to follow up

training them," Craig concludes. "This is the key to our success."

Training is a key to every top producer's success, and that includes training your Associates to train their own Associates to train their Associates, and so on. The process continues indefinitely, and that is how you multiply your success many times over!

> **Secrets of the Top Producers**
> **"If you throw information out there, follow back up on it."**
> -*Dave Savula, Dawsonville, GA*

The benefits of follow-up

Following up is simply re-contacting the prospects you have already exposed to Pre-Paid Legal and making another exposure. Follow-up also includes keeping in contact with the Associates you help bring into the business.

Understanding the benefits of following up will help motivate you to follow up.

Benefit #1—fortune is in the follow-up

You will hear it again and again because it's true: "Fortune is in the follow-up!" For example, within 24 to 48 hours of your prospects receiving a video/CD-ROM in the mail, you need to be calling them while the information is still fresh in their minds.

In fact, when you first call to say a package is on its way, you should set a specific time for you to call back so that you aren't playing voicemail tag. Then call precisely when you say you will call. If they have watched it, you go to the next exposure (3-way call, sending them to your website, recorded message, etc.). If they haven't watched it, reset a time to call them back. Until they have watched the video/CD and decided they are not interested at this time, you still have an open door.

Only rarely (1 out of 100) do people buy a membership or become an Associate on the first exposure. Every exposure after the first one is considered follow-up, and since the other 99 sales are waiting for you, your fortune is clearly in the follow-up.

Benefit #2—teamwork is in the follow-up

Whoever defined TEAM as Together Everyone Achieves More was right on the money! Only in a team can you build a level of trust and friendship that will enable everyone to reach his or her goals.

When you take the time to follow up (call, email, train, go to events together, make presentations together, use the ROMAR forms in your *Success Planner*, etc.) with the Associates you've brought into the business, you get to know them and are able to help maximize their abilities. Top producer Steve Fleming explains, "If I can find your unique strengths, that is what I'm going to focus on instead of trying to teach you my skill. I take your unique talents and try to work that into the business, which is basically a way to show you how to be financially independent and create a residual income."

The benefit, Steve adds, is that "when you build a strong team, everyone is building and accomplishing their dreams." Everyone achieves more and everyone wins! That is only possible in a team.

Following up with your Associates is not only necessary, it's good business. Top producer Tom Wood tells his new Associates when they are making their list of 100 names, "Give me the names of

The Player's Club

Rewards: recognition, prizes, a monthly car bonus, and an annual trip

Requirements: 5 points each month through any of following combinations:

♦ Recruit a new Fast Start Associate = **2 points**

♦ Sell a non-group membership = **1 point**

♦ Sell a Business Owners Legal Solution Plan ($69-$150) = **2 points**

♦ Open a new group account (with 5 or more members) = **1 point**

♦ Sell 5 group memberships = **1 point**

For more information, see playersclub@pplsi.com

20 people who you are totally afraid to call or you think would never get into the business and I'll call them for you." By doing this, Tom is helping build his Associates' business and thereby his own.

One of the best ways to see if everyone is actively working toward their goals is to ask if each person has qualified that month for Pre-Paid Legal's Player's Club. This innovative program encourages constant growth through membership sales and recruiting and offers rewards, bonuses, and a yearly all-expense-paid cruise for every Associate who qualifies each month in a calendar year!

In every respect, follow-up will benefit you and your team.

Benefit #3—personal growth and development is in the follow-up

Countless people have been touched by Associates who cared enough to reach out to them, encourage them, and believe in them. This is what top producers do with the Associates they help bring into the business. As a result, beliefs change, attitudes change, and lives change.

Top producers Frank and Theresa AuCoin are clear in this respect when they say to their new Associates, "Our first concern is setting up a financial firewall around you and your family in case you couldn't work, the money would still be coming into your house." That is powerful! But for most people, additional personal growth and development is required before they can reach their goals.

Mike and Steve Melia, brothers, partners, and two of Pre-Paid Legal's top producers, understood this before they had any success in the business. Mike says, "We always got to events early and stayed late so we could hang out with the people who were the movers and shakers. We weren't top players, but we hung out with them anyway."

> **Homerun!**
> #11.1—Helping an Associate get his or her first sale

But hanging out wasn't enough. "We also bought the tapes and books of certain people and made their information part of our lives, thus making them one of our top influences," Mike explains. "We didn't have much personal time with these authors and speakers, but we listened to their tapes over and over. It reinforced what we wanted in our lives."

It wasn't long before Mike and Steve became what they were preparing to be—top producers.

Benefit #4—residual income is in the follow-up

As you know, you make money in Pre-Paid Legal through:

  a) personal sales
  b) organizational overrides
  c) training bonuses
  d) residual income

Personal sales, overrides, and bonuses come at the time of the sale, but your residual income will continue as long as your memberships remain in force. To help guarantee your residual income, follow-up with those members is an absolute must.

Top producer Brian Carruthers insightfully states, "When a person decides to get started and signs the application, that is simply their permission for you to keep recruiting them." With Associates, this makes perfect sense, but it also makes perfect sense with those who bought a membership.

Practically speaking, you can only follow up directly with a limited number of people, so how are you supposed to follow up with the increasing number of people who purchase a membership from you? Or, since this is residual income

> **Secrets of the Top Producers**
> "We are keeping people plugged in, communicating to them, and constantly training them. This is the key to our success."
> -Craig Hepner, Newport Beach, CA

we are talking about, how do you keep the business on the books?

Pre-Paid Legal knows you can't possibly call all those with memberships and ask how they like the service, if they've taken care of their Will, and why they aren't using their attorney more. It would be great if you could as it would drastically reduce the number of people canceling their membership and you receiving a chargeback (a pro-rated amount deducted from your commissions when a membership cancels before the 3-year advance is earned out), but there is not enough time in a day to do so. That is why Pre-Paid Legal recommends the services of Integrity Resource Management, a company

Follow through to follow up

that specializes in handling this part of your business (www.integrity4you.com or call 1-888-272-0986).

Integrity Resource Management makes 2 personal phone calls to each of your members and Associates to see if they are using their membership, if they have any questions, and if they are satisfied with the service. Integrity Resource

> Secrets of the Top Producers
> "You must inspect what you expect-first yourself, then those around you."
> -Paul J. Meyer, Waco, TX

Management also follows up by sending out 3 letters per year per person with your name, address, etc. on it. You get quarterly reports on membership activity, you are notified of members who are about to cancel, and leads/referrals are obtained from willing members. All that for a mere $8.50 per member per year!

Top producer Michael Clouse believes strongly in the service because of the dramatic decrease in cancellations he and his team have experienced. "This business is not about getting someone to buy a membership," he points out, "it is about someone keeping the membership."

Follow-up does indeed affect your bottom line—for years and years to come!

Plan-Do-Review

As you keep your Plan of Action in focus and steadily walk toward your goals, it is vitally important that you pause occasionally to review your progress.

♦ Are you making the daily number of exposures that you planned?

♦ Are there distractions you face that can be avoided?

♦ Are you avoiding one aspect of the business, as top producer John Hoffman asks, because of "fear of the phone, fear of rejection, fear of what people will say, or fear of what your spouse thinks?"

♦ You may even be sailing toward your success without a problem, but could you be going a little faster?

However you would rate your performance, it is important that you start with your personal progress, then you can work with your Associates on what might be slowing down their success. Top producer Frank AuCoin found that what throws a lot of new Associates off track is the fact that they are not plugged into the communication systems that Pre-Paid Legal provides. Whatever the case may be, pausing to review will do wonders.

Pre-Paid Legal's *Success Planner* will help tremendously in this area. At the end of every month is a list of steps designed to help re-focus your efforts for the following month. Some of the monthly steps include:

♦ Identifying your most important personal and business goals

♦ Prioritizing your top personal and business goals and identifying your high payoff activities

♦ Completing Goal Planning Sheets on your top personal and business goals as needed

♦ Setting up a tracking method to measure your goals and high payoff activities

♦ Scheduling blocks of time for your goals and high payoff activities

When it comes time to Plan-Do-Review, Pre-Paid Legal provides top-quality tools and materials that are tailor-made for your success!

Communication with new Associates

Another top producer, Bill Carter, takes this Plan-Do-Review process so seriously that he has the Associates on his team who are actively working toward their goals be part of what he calls a "Structure Call." Three times a month, near the 1st, the 15th, and the 25th of each month, 8 Associates (i.e. a director and his/her team of managers, and Executive Director and his/her team of directors, etc.) get together on a conference call to discuss their progress.

This is the process that Bill takes his team through each month:

On the 1st I ask if they are committed to the Player's Club. If so, then this is for them. I ask what their pay structure is and what their goal is by the end of the month. Whatever that goal is, we put a Game Plan together for them. Then I ask them what they want to earn this month, what they will do with that money (the money has to have a WHY behind it for them to have an emotional attachment to their goal) and what their memberships and recruits goals are.

On the 15th we review. If they make their goals, we congratulate them.

On the 25th, we review again. If they are just short, we ask how they can reach their goals, and then they commit to whatever is necessary to reach that goal before the month ends.

Such a system breeds accountability, team-work, and success. The basis, Bill explains, is about "keeping us on track." From experience, he knows that those who stay on track will hit the mark!

> **Homerun!**
> #11.2—Reviewing regularly your goals and your progress

When you take the time to review your progress, you will inevitably see that you can improve in one or more areas. You are in good company, because every top producer in Pre-Paid Legal is in the same boat! Nobody has arrived.

We can always get better, make more sales, recruit more Associates, help more people, etc., and that is precisely the importance of following through to follow up.

Follow through to follow up

Steps To Ensure Personal Success
Chapter #11

1. **Practice** following through and following up

2. **Focus on training**—first yourself, then others

3. Act upon the truth that **"Fortune is in the follow-up"**

4. **Follow up** with those on your team

5. Qualify for the **Player's Club** every month

6. Pursue **personal growth** and **development**

7. Guarantee your **residual income** through proper follow-up

8. **Review** your progress and the progress of your team—**every month**

Follow through to follow up

> Secrets of the Top Producers
> "We have to slow down and educate and train and mentor the individuals we bring into the business."
> -Michael Clouse, Lynnwood, WA

PART IV

TRAINING FOR
CONTINUED SUCCESS

This business is about finding people to talk to, talking to those people, and teachings those who join you to do the same. Between finding people to talk to and teaching them to do the same, if there is a breakdown, your level of success will slow down.

The answer is to continually pay attention to the little details. If your presentation needs a little work, work on it. Likewise with your prospecting, getting referrals, recruiting, and duplicating. Invest time and study into these key areas on a monthly basis and your success will only increase!

Kevin Rhea, president of L-K Marketing Group

Chapter #12 reveals:

- How to never make cold calls again!

- The mindset of a prospector

- 7 ways to create a flow of non-stop prospects

- How to track your prospects

"Justice For All"

PROSPECTING

Zachary, an apartment manager in Miami, happened to be at home when the phone rang. "Hi Zach, this is Jeff Graham. It's been several years since we took classes together at the University of Florida. Remember me?"

"Uh, yeah." Zachary said, slowly putting the name with a face. "How are you? What are you doing?"

Jeff replied, "I'm doing great! I'm working part-time for an incredible New York Stock Exchange company that provides pre-paid legal coverage, much like medical insurance covering hospital bills, and the business is expanding in Miami and I need your help. I know you might not be interested in the service or the business opportunity, but I was really wondering if you would help introduce me to some influential people whom I might otherwise not get a chance to meet."

"Sure, I'd be glad to help, but I'm not the best at coming up with names on the spot," Zachary responded.

Jeff said, "That's fine, I can help you with the names. Did you play golf this past weekend—who did you play with? What's your barber's name? Did you go out to eat last week with any business associates—who were they? What's your accountant's name? What company do you hire to advertise your apartments?"

"You had better grab a pen, because I have a ton of names to give you," Zachary joked. "Ready?"

With that, and a few more questions, Jeff was able to get more than 25 names of people who knew and trusted Zachary (thus an automatic open door) and who had their own circles of influence. And if each of these people knew just 10 more people, Jeff would have 250 additional quality prospects! And if those knew 5 people each . . .

Prospecting is the name of the game

Years ago, while in the life insurance business, I coined the phrase, "I would rather be a master prospector than the wizard of speech and have no one to tell my story to!" As a result, I set a goal back then to:

1. Never depend on leads from advertising
2. Never depend on leads from the company
3. Never to make "cold calls"
4. Never be "appointment broke" each morning

Did it work? Well, I'll let you decide:

♦ At age 19—I led the largest weekly premium insurance company in the nation!
♦ At age 21—I led the largest exclusive ordinary life insurance agency in the nation!
♦ At age 23—I qualified as the youngest life member of the Million Dollar Round Table.
♦ At age 24—I owned more life insurance on my own life than any other top producer in America...with any company.
♦ At age 25—I built the largest life insurance agency in the country and recruited 820 sales people in 12 months!

♦ At age 25—I was the highest paid insurance salesman in the country

♦ And I conducted hundreds of seminars for life insurance agencies on "how to prospect your way to millions"

Suffice to say, prospecting works—***and it still does!***

The mindset of a prospector

Finding prospects to present Pre-Paid Legal to is clearly the goal, but where do you find prospects? The answer is simple: every person living and breathing is a prospect!

When this idea is firmly implanted in your head, you will be amazed at how differently every-one appears. Before long, your new insight, attitude, and belief about people will create an even more remark-able change—a totally

> **Homerun!**
> #12.1—Making prospecting your most important goal in Pre-Paid Legal

altered reaction toward what you had heretofore considered "just a crowd."

The people you see in cars, on the sidewalks, in the theaters, at restaurants, and in sports arenas will no longer be anonymous faceless masses. Rather, you will see them all as prospective Pre-Paid Legal members and Associates.

Here is something even more important: once you establish this truth—that people are prospects and prospects are people—you will notice an even greater change in yourself: ***prospecting will now be of paramount importance!***

You instinctively and intuitively will be arranging your day, your time, and your life to see

Prospecting

and talk to more and more new people until it becomes a dynamic drive, a force, and an obsession. When this happens, you are well on your way to permanent success in Pre-Paid Legal.

I have observed many companies spend an enormous amount of money teaching their sales people and marketing consultants all sorts of skills and abilities: how to dress, how to act, the history of the company, how to make sales presentations with high-tech equipment, etc.

Frankly, it is a waste of time! *Improving talent is meaningless without mastering the art of prospecting.* In other words, you must develop a continuous flow of people to expose to Pre-Paid Legal or you will end up falling far short of success.

The answer is to make prospecting your most important goal in Pre-Paid Legal! You started toward this goal when you made your initial list of 100 to 200 names of people to contact, but eventually you will go through those names. What you need is a system for ongoing prospects, and to get

> When your prospecting awareness, prospecting consciousness, and prospecting attitude become a prospecting habit—**watch out!**

that, you must first have a prospecting awareness.

The 4-step formula to developing a prospecting awareness

Prospecting is a matter of talking to the right people at the right time under favorable circumstances. With that, the bottom line must be first: there are only two kinds of prospects—those you know and those you don't know. Or you could say it another way: there are only two kinds of

Prospecting

prospects—those who are Pre-Paid Legal members and those who are not.

To make this reality a practical and financial benefit to you, you must develop your prospecting awareness. Here are the 4 steps to do so:

Step #1—expect Class-A prospects to enter your life. Class-A prospects are people who want a membership, who would be great recruits, or who have a lot of referrals for you. When you expect them, they will come, even when you least expect it.

Step #2—see Class-A prospects everywhere. You need to further define what a Class-A prospect looks like. When you first start, a Class-A prospect may be anyone within 3 feet of you. As you get more experienced, you will narrow that down to a type of person whom you do a better job with. Every person relates to others differently, so what might be a Class-A to me might not be to you, and vice versa. Define it for yourself, then tune in and you will find exactly what you are looking for.

Step #3—believe that you have a service that people want and need. When you believe you have what people want, they will enter your life. They will seek you out, or at least you will find them and offer it to them. The only way they will know is if you or one of your Associates tells them.

Step #4—set a goal to never, never, never use a directory or list. Lists and directories are last resorts—fill-ins. To really develop a prospecting awareness, you need to talk to people you know and people they know. Using

Prospecting

directories or lists as your main source of prospects will cripple your prospecting ability.

Creating a flow of non-stop prospects

From a prospecting awareness, you need to springboard into a system that will create a flow of non-stop prospects. In other words, dig the well before you thirst. The need for water (needing prospects) is obvious, but having a well (a steady flow of prospects) is what will cata- pult your Pre-Paid Legal busi- ness beyond what you ever imagined possible!

> **Homerun!**
> #12.2—Becoming a master prospector

Here are 7 methods for creating the non-stop flow of prospects that you need:

#1—Centers of influence

A center of influence is someone who <u>consis- tently</u> sends people to you whom you <u>sell</u> (member- ship or recruit). People will give you referrals and people will give you sales, but a true center of influ- ence is someone who will continue to do this on a regular basis. ***This is a very valuable commodity!***

Systematically find centers of influence. Using someone's help to increase your business is called leverage and is usually in that person's spe- cific area of influence, such as:

- ◆ social influence
- ◆ civic influence
- ◆ leadership in general
- ◆ geographical influence
- ◆ financial influence (banker, accountant, etc.)
- ◆ spiritual influence (pastor, priest, etc.)
- ◆ political influence

Prospecting

♦ business/industry influence

A center of influence is sold on you and/or on what you are doing. Knowing you are a person of integrity and character is powerful, but if he or she does not know or understand what it is you are selling, you might not get a referral. When your center of influence

> **Secrets of the Top Producers**
> "When I'm prospecting, I try to be more interested in them than trying to be interesting myself."
> *-Ed Parker, Flower Mound, TX*

believes in you **and** your service, you are much more likely to be referred.

You might be wondering, "Just how am I supposed to find a center a influence?" When your prospecting awareness is heightened, you will naturally find centers of influence. However, finding centers of influence is not the whole story; you need to **develop** centers of influence.

Centers of influence—how to develop them:

#1—make a list of centers of influence. Then separate them into 2 categories: A) people you know and they know you or B) people you know or know of, but they don't know you. There are a lot of people in powerful positions who have a lot of influence, but they don't know you. You can, however, get a recommendation.

#2—prioritize the list. Depending on how well you know the person, how much leverage/influence they have, and how much they relate to you and/or what you are doing, prioritize the list. You are basically ranking them

Prospecting

on how good of a job they will do to help you build your business. List from best to worst.

#3—develop a Plan of Action for each center of influence. Set up a separate file/notebook for each person. Develop a Plan of Action for each person. Those in Category-A (you know them) you contact directly, while those in Category-B (you know of them) you contact indirectly. Part of this will involve getting to know the person. In the proper care and feeding of a center of influence, you want to show an interest in that person and that person to show an interest in you. You want to know that person's likes and dislikes, hobbies, family, etc. Gravitate toward knowing more about them and do special things for them from time to time. The more you know about him/her, the better they will treat you.

#4—contact potential centers of influence in priority order. Make contact with your best centers of influence first. Go to that person, explain the concept behind Pre-Paid Legal, how you make sales and recruits, some of the benefits to members, etc.

#5—ask him or her for help. People really want to help if you are sincere about it. Ask for help! Be specific as well. Say something to the effect of, "I'd like you to be my silent partner" or "I'd like you to introduce me to people I otherwise might not know" or "You have a lot of influence in this arena and I know you are proud of that and it's taken you years to build. I'll be very professional and discreet in contacting these people just as I have been with you. I just want to borrow some of the

Prospecting

trust that you have built up over the years."
Ask for the help!

Centers of influence—how to help them help you:

Be even more specific about what a Class-A prospect looks like. You have defined a Class-A prospect already as someone wanting the service, the opportunity, having referrals, or as someone with whom you get along. Now take the next step and define this certain type of person to your center of influence. If your Class-A prospects are often seasoned insurance salespeople or accountants looking for part-time work, then say just that. And as you describe your Class-A prospects to your center of influence,

> Secrets of the Top Producers
> "The only reason you aren't making enough sales as you would like to and are capable of is simply because you aren't seeing enough people at the right time."
> -Paul J. Meyer, Waco, TX

go ahead and ask for leads in certain towns or sections of town. Zero in. Be specific. It will save you time!

When you begin to make contact with these leads, be sure to give your centers of influence feedback. Let them know when you've made contact, what the person bought, how the service/opportunity is benefiting them, etc. Periodically a hand-written note is great, such as, "Janice of company X has used the service twice, not to mention getting her Will done. She is pleased that you introduced me to her. Thank you." That will make your center of influence want to do it again. Give them feedback if the referral doesn't buy either. Thank them and say something like, "I appreciate you giving me her name. She was too busy at the time, but I'll check back with her later."

Make your center of influence aware of your accomplishments in Pre-Paid Legal (Player's Club, recognition in *Connection* magazine, etc.). Make extra copies of what you were recognized for, then write a note on it, such as, "Thank you for your help. I was recently recognized for my efforts. Your help means a lot to me!" and sign it.

Also, show an interest in your centers of influence in unusual ways. For example, if you see an article in a magazine that pertains to their hobby/interest, cut it out and mail it to them. Send them a small gift, such as a framed picture. Show them courtesy, but don't try to buy them or tip them for all their help.

#2—Referrals

The second method for creating a non-stop flow of prospects is through the use of referrals. Referrals are similar to centers of influence in that you are borrowing the influence and trust of the person who referred you and getting a good reception because of it. This is what leverage is all about.

Keep in mind that the best people to get referrals from are those who just bought a membership from you. They have confidence in you and in your company, so make sure you ask for referrals.

A new member or friend may give you referrals from time to time, but a center of influence will do it regularly. You can get referrals from centers of influence, clients, prospects, friends,

> **Homerun!**
> #12.3—Developing a
> prospecting awareness

acquaintances, business associates, etc. (A proven approach to getting referrals is explained in more detail in Chapter #14.)

#3—Observation

This is the third method for creating a non-stop flow of prospects and in some instances it's even better than referrals and centers of influence because observation is based on first-hand knowledge. For example, you can usually tell successful people by the neighborhoods they live in, the cars they drive, how they dress, how they walk, how they talk, where they eat, etc.

The more you get accustomed to keying in on successful people, the more easily you will spot them. What is a successful person? Someone who is progressively realizing pre-determined worthwhile personal goals. It doesn't mean he or she is the richest person in town. Someone who is fulfilled and reaching goals in every area of life—that person is successful.

Get your antennas up and be alert for successful people. Look for people recently promoted, companies hiring management level personal, businesses that are expanding, etc. This type of information is often right in the newspaper.

Be curious. Keep eyes and ears open. Professional eavesdropping works well, especially when you say, "I'm sorry to eavesdrop, but I heard

Prospecting

you say . . .", then follow up right then with them or write the information down and follow up later. Knowledge gives you leverage. Wilburn Smith, President of Pre-Paid Legal, often says, "You drive by more business in a day than you could handle in a year." Well said, so look at the signs along the road, in the newspaper, on trucks, etc.

Be observant because your prospects are everywhere!

#4—Speaking engagements

Another method for non-stop prospects includes making yourself available for speaking engagements, but not without first getting a list of names, whether it's the membership list or attendance list. You can also collect business cards, use a drawing, etc. but just make sure you don't leave without getting a list of individuals or businesses represented by those in attendance.

If an organization or group meets once a month, they need 12 speakers, and if twice a month, they need 24 speakers. It's easy to become one of the speakers, and they would appreciate it.

To prepare, develop one flexible speech that can go from 20 minutes to 40 minutes, depending on how much time they give you. Then you will be prepared to make a presentation anywhere.

#5—Develop nests or vertical markets

Having non-stop prospects comes from gaining entrance into one business that has multiple other businesses related to it. For example, the food industry has restaurants, wholesalers, grocers, processors, suppliers, etc. There are dozens of companies in such a nest.

Prospecting

Use nests or vertical markets as a way of gaining prospects and referrals.

#6—Drop-bys or fill-ins

Drop-bys or fill-ins are also ways to create a flow of prospects. When you have time, you can "drop by" a business simply to learn and listen as you look for Class-A prospects. The least that could happen when you stop by is that you find out about the business, how they operate, the atmosphere, how friendly the employees are, the boss's name, who owns it, manager's name, and maybe even schedule an appointment.

> **5 affirmations to make your own!**
> 1. I am a master prospector.
> 2. I see prospects everywhere.
> 3. I have 10 centers of influence and they are making me rich.
> 4. I ask for and receive 8 referrals on every sales call.
> 5. I get prospects at every speaking engagement.
>
> *Affirmations are statements stated positively with pronoun "I" and always in present tense that should be on your office wall, in your wallet, and in your* Success *Planner*

When you show genuine interest, there are few people who will turn you down.

#7—Lists and directories

The last method for creating a non-stop flow of prospects is that of lists and directories. These are often found in newspapers, libraries, magazines, journals, etc. The number of quality leads will of course be less than what a center of influence would provide you with, but there are still prospects hidden within the lists.

Always work where you get the best results, such as with your centers of influence, but running

Prospecting

lists and directories as a steady "background" method will occasionally give you results.

Track your prospects with a proven system

If you can measure it, you can manage it. With the prospects flowing non-stop to you, it is vitally important that you track each one. Here is a proven system that will enable you to manage your prospects:

I.   write each prospect's name on an individual 3x5 card

II. classify each card as an A, B, or C, with A being the best prospect and most likely to buy and C being the least likely

III. learn the "salesperson + prospect = sale" formula (Every sale equals a 10, so if you are start ing out in the business and you are a level-3 salesperson, you need a level-7prospect to make a sale: 7+3=10. That is why you call on better prospects first. With experience, you become a level-5 salesperson and can handle level-5 prospects. Finally, when you are a level-10 salesperson, you can handle those who don't even want to buy. If you are a level-8 and you call on a level-8 prospect, you have a very high chance for a sale.)

IV. organize your 3x5 cards from A to C

V.   schedule an appointment with your prospect (level-A first)

VI. make presentation and make sale

VII. get referrals from your new friend and Pre-Paid Legal member/Associate

VIII. repeat this cycle from the top

How to never make cold calls again

I once hired a man who approached his 60 best friends and amazingly made 60 sales, but soon after he quit the business because he had no more prospects! Never once did he ask for a referral, a prospect, or even a recommendation from any of the 60 people. Do not ever let this happen to you!

Pre-Paid Legal offers an incredible service and opportunity, making it easy to ask for referrals. Do so and you will always be in business. Do so and you will always have quality leads to call on, just like my farmer friend from Louisiana I recruited into the insurance business. At one point he had 5,000 referrals that he hadn't even contacted yet!

How did he get so many leads? He was motivated by fear—he was scared that he would run out of leads! He didn't want to make cold calls or run ads so badly that when he finished selling, he would spend more time getting referrals than he did making the sale. He found out everything about the referrals, including personality type, number of children, color favorites, style of clothing, political views, shoe type, alma mater, sports interests, attitude, family, religious beliefs, hair style, car choice, home owner or renter, age, etc. He was incredible!

I doubt he ever contacted all the leads he generated himself, but that sure beats sitting nervously in front of the telephone with a phone book! There is, however, a time and a place for making cold calls, but it should only be for a short season in your sales career.

> **Secrets of the Top Producers**
> "The secret is to always work your warm market. You'll never run out of leads!"
> -Mike Melia, Atlanta, GA

201

People say, "I don't like making cold calls—how can I do it more effectively?" My response is simple, "Why make cold calls at all?" When you make prospecting your focus, there will come a day when you will have so many prospects that you won't ever need to make a cold call again! Wouldn't that be terrible!

Top producer Mike Melia understands this concept very clearly. Listen to his logic as he shows the power of prospecting through new Associates:

The average person can come up with 100 names. We then prioritize it down to 20 top prospects. Put these 20 through the process of exposure and on average 3 of them will become Associates. We then train these 3 new Associates to contact their top 20, which gives us a total of 80 top-20 prospects, 400 individuals total. When these 3 Associates get 3 new Associate each, we have 260 top-20 names and 1300 names all together! It's a simple system.

However you meet people, they always know a lot of other people. If each of the new Associates were to get 3 more Associates, we would have a total of 40 Associates with 800 top-20 prospects and 4,000 individuals total. In this type of warm market, you'll never run out of people to talk to.

The real name for all sales is prospecting, the name of selling is prospecting, and the foundation for every successful sale is prospecting. Prospecting is the only way any of us hope to succeed in sales. You've got to develop a prospecting awareness, a prospecting consciousness, and a prospecting con-

Prospecting

cept. You've got to dive in and immerse yourself. You've got to saturate yourself from your toenails to your eyeballs with one idea—one obsession—above all else...prospecting.

Why? Because success in selling has only one name, and the name of the game is prospecting.

Steps To Ensure Personal Success
Chapter #12

1.. Learn to **see everyone as a prospect**

2. Internalize the 4-step process for **developing a prospecting awareness**:
   Step #1—expect Class-A prospects to enter your life
   Step #2—see Class-A prospects everywhere
   Step #3—believe that you have a service that people want and need
   Step #4—set a goal to never, never, never use a directory or list

3. Allow your prospecting awareness, prospecting consciousness, and prospecting attitude to become a **prospecting habit**

4. Learn how to simultaneously **develop** centers of influence, referrals, observations, speaking engagements, nests and vertical markets, drop-bys and fill-ins, and lists and directories

5. Use a proven system to **track your prospects**

6. Remember that success in sales is spelled **p-r-o-s-p-e-c-t-i-n-g**

> Secrets of the Top Producers
> "I would rather be a master prospec-tor than a wizard of speech and have no one to tell my story to."
> -Paul J. Meyer, Waco, TX

Prospecting

Chapter #13 reveals:

- Why sorting is always better than selling

- How to prepare for your presentation

- The #1 skill in presenting

- How to handle rejection from anyone

"Justice For All"

PRESENTING

"Excuse me, how long have you worked here?" Kim asks an individual working in a store. "I couldn't help but notice how great you were with these people. You have a great outgoing personality. The reason I'm mentioning it is because I'm with a national company that is expanding in this area and we are looking for a couple people like you who would like to earn a few hundred to a few thousand dollars a week part-time and maybe even more full-time. If you could earn that kind of income and fit it in with what you are doing, would that have some interest to you?"

Everyone is interested.

Kim continues, "Do you have a cassette player in your car?" Most do. "Will you listen to this cassette on your way home?" The answer is usually positive. "What's your home number? Here's mine. If I haven't heard from you by the time I get home, I'll give you a call, fair enough?"

When the individual arrives home, Kim calls and says, "What did you like best?"

From there Kim puts the person on a 3-way call with her sponsor (or some other "expert" in Pre-Paid Legal), invites the individual to a meeting, or schedules a 1-on-1 meeting. As Kim moves people through a series of exposures, some buy a membership and some become recruits.

Presenting

Sorting instead of selling

This is the approach that Kim learned from her sponsor. It worked with her and it's working with other people. She realizes that it is important to qualify her prospects **before** she takes them to the next step of giving them a tool

> **Homerun!**
>
> #13.1—Asking yourself: "Everybody can be sold by somebody, why not me?"

(an audiocassette in this case). The result of taking a few seconds to qualify her prospects is that more of them purchase a membership or become Associates.

Kim is sorting, not selling. If the person isn't interested, she moves on to another prospect. Other qualifying questions include:

- ◆ Do you have an interest in earning an additional income?
- ◆ Do you ever look at other business opportunities?
- ◆ Is this what you want to do for the rest of your life?

You should ask these types of questions **first** because you are really trying to find out what your prospects want. Then, **second**, you will show them how to get it. If they don't want it (the membership or the opportunity), your showing them how to get it will fall on deaf ears.

Top producer Ken Smith discerningly states, "A person convinced against their will is of the same opinion still." In other words, as he says, "This is more about sorting than selling."

That is the reason why he focuses on exposing people to Pre-Paid Legal without spending a lot of time, money, and effort trying to sell them some-

Presenting

thing. He and his team use recorded phone messages, while others use CD-ROMs, audiocassettes, or videos. Each is effective, but the use of the tools is based on making an exposure and not on forcing a sale.

> Secrets of the Top Producers
> "I've learned to use the tools and be the messenger, not the message."
> -Ken Smith, Vancouver, B.C. Canada

Every top producer has learned what it means to sort instead of sell, but this does not mean they aren't prepared with an effective presentation. The secret, after you have asked qualifying questions, is to:

A. know what to say
B. know whom to say it to
C. and then go out and say it

And all that requires preparation.

Preparation *before* presentation

I have witnessed many disastrous presentations over the years from well-educated people. They had an excellent product or a good service, but they began their presentation half prepared, with half the materials arranged in the wrong sequence... fumbling...groping...looking and sounding unprofessional.

Prior planning prevents poor performance. It always has and it always will.

I always learn about the prospects themselves. If they are referred leads, I learn everything possible about them, including their family, hobbies, interests, work, goals in life, how they think, etc. This is all part of preparing to make a presentation.

I also always double-check my materials and handouts I need for my presentation. I have learned that my own attitude in the presentation is equally as important as my professional preparation. I ask myself:

♦ How am I entering into this presentation—as a giver or a taker?
♦ Am I going into this presentation to dominate or to serve?
♦ Am I going into it to tell and sell or to listen and see a need and show how my service can fill that need?

I also check my:

♦ Excitement
♦ Emotion
♦ Enthusiasm
♦ Self-image
♦ Self-esteem
♦ Self-confidence

> **Luck is where opportunity and preparation meet!**

Then I believe with all my heart and soul that the person I call on has been waiting to see me, meet me, and do business with me all of his or her life. And because I am prepared and I am offering a service that he or she wants and needs, I believe:

1. I have earned the right to see this person.
2. I am professionally and mentally prepared.
3. I have the appointment.
4. I will make the sale!
5. I win!
6. My prospect wins!
7. We both have another great day!

But I don't want to get so excited that I forget to obtain some referral leads from my new client.

After all, I have just lost my very best prospect. That person is now a member or Associate and has become my best source to get another one just like him or her! And because I am an optimist, this new

> **Homerun!**
> #13.2—Building rapport

referral may be an even better prospect!

Selling is easy when you are prepared.

The #1 skill for presenting

Every top producer has one thing in common: great people skills. Top producer Tom Wood defines this ability "to get someone to trust you, like you, and want to do business with you" as rapport.

Everyone has the same tools, compensation plan, events, etc., but what is different is your relationship with the people you make a presentation to. This means respecting where someone is coming from, no matter where it is, and being responsive to his or her needs and wants. "If you can do that," says Tom, "whether it's face-to-face, over the phone, or online, the other person is going to trust you and is much more likely to do business with you."

The benefits of rapport are clear, but how do you practically build rapport? Tom explains:

> When someone is talking to you, you need to have these two questions constantly in mind: "What can I appreciate about this person?" and "What can I understand about this person?" Once somebody says something, what you need to do is stop and think back to a point where you used to think that same thing. Respond by saying, "I can appreciate that because I used to think that too" or

Presenting

"I can appreciate that because I know other people who felt that way."

When you think this way, the first words that come out of your mouth are not, "I have the greatest opportunity in the world where you can make all the money you want," but rather, "Tell me a little bit about your background" or "Tell me what kind of income you are looking for." You are showing interest and trust builds.

If you stop and look at it, rapport is simply listening and serving the other person. Simple, yes, but more powerful than you ever imagined!

How to handle rejection

The goal is always to expose as many people as you can to Pre-Paid Legal with hopes that they will want the service/opportunity. To do that, every prospect must first be willing to review the information. In essence, "you are asking for their help," says top producer John Hoffman,

> **Secrets of the Top Producers**
> "If you talk to nobody, you'll make no money, if you talk to a few people, you'll make a little bit of money, if you talk to a lot of people, you'll make a lot of money."
> -Ed Parker, Flower Mound, TX

"and anyone will help you since they aren't being asked to join or being offered another scam of a deal."

It's a pretty easy approach—exposing rather than selling—and it's a win-win for sure. But despite the soft-sell approach, receiving a "no" is hard for new Associates to handle. "Learn to love massive rejection," offers top producer Ed Parker, "because to have massive success, you must go through massive rejection."

This rejection can cause call reluctance, which is the result of being afraid that the person on the line is going to strike back and hurt you. Everyone wants to be liked, loved, appreciated, and wanted. That is how we are made, so making a phone call with the fear that you won't be loved, liked, etc., is what turns many people

> **Homerun!**
> #13.3—Learning to love massive rejection

away from it. The usual approach is to protect ourselves by making excuses for not picking up the phone.

Of the 15,000+ sales calls I've made, I had my fill of "no" answers, but I've never been hurt. That is because they can't physically hurt me over the phone and because I understand how not to take it personally.

The secret to handling rejection is in understanding the IR-Theory:

- ♦ I—who you are as an individual
- ♦ R—who you are in your role

You have many roles, such as parent, teacher, salesperson, spouse, politician, etc. In that role, you are critiqued or rated on what you do, how you perform, your results, etc.

Most people rate themselves in the same way. On a scale of 1 to 10, they rate themselves low, between 4 and 6. The fact is that no matter what anyone says or does, I am a 10 and that will not and can not change. I don't give anyone permission to affect the "I" in who I am. My performance through my role, however, is a different story.

Presenting

When people let what affects them in their role affect them in who they are, damage comes quickly. The man at work, for example, who has a bad day because his boss chewed him out is fuming on the way home. He sits down in his recliner and yells at his kids, complains about dinner, refuses to participate, etc. What is happening? He is letting what affected him in his role affect him in who he is, but this is nothing but a downward spiral.

If he felt like a 4 that morning, after his boss's comments he felt like a 2. People who reach bottom do abusive and illogical things. They hurt themselves, drink, steal, become lazy, give up on their dreams, and quit.

> Secrets of the Top Producers
> **"The #1 skill is your ability to get along with people."**
> -Frank AuCoin, Charleston, SC

They do this because they believe **I**dentity and **R**ole are the same thing, but they are not!

Never let what happens in your role affect what happens in your identity. The phone fear cannot affect your identity because your role has nothing to do with your identity. You are born a 10 and you are a 10 tomorrow. Don't let anyone put you down.

As a result of believing this, I've gone back into the same office that turned me away the day before and said, "I know I didn't make a sale yesterday, but do you mind telling me what I did wrong? Was I too quick, slow, unclear, too intense, did I not listen, etc.?" I could do that because my role is not my identity. I asked my clients what I did right or wrong and learned a lot. I figured if I made one less mistake everyday, I was sure to succeed.

Getting past fears and inhibitions is all about attitude.

The attitude behind your presentation

An introvert, mild, soft-spoken individual—so soft-spoken that you couldn't hear him—decided that he wanted to sell for one of my companies. It was utterly illogical!

He started selling and did 200 presentations **without a sale!** His attitude remained positive and he continued to say that he was on a learning curve. I honestly thought he should quit and go do something else, but he persisted. He ended up being the highest paid sales person I ever had, making over a million dollars a year!

His secret was that he saw each presentation as better than the one before it. It was a good thing he believed that so strongly, because he had the worst start of anyone who has worked for me in more than 50 years out of hundreds of thousands of sales people.

Top producer Mike Melia explains it a slightly different way: "I was in the front row at an event when Dave Savula, who was making close to a million dollars a year in Pre-Paid Legal at the time, said, 'The only difference between me and you is that I've done thousands of meetings.' I decided right then and there that I would make thousands of presentations." And Mike's business is booming today!

When you mix preparation with an I-will-not-quit attitude and cap it off with an I-am-getting-better-with-every-presentation perspective, Pre-Paid Legal had better watch out because you are coming through!

Steps To Ensure Personal Success
Chapter #13

1. Understand that you need to **sort, not sell**

2. Ask **qualifying questions** up front

3. **Be prepared** before you present

4. **Check your attitude** before your next presentation. Are you:
   - ♦ Entering into this presentation as a giver or a taker?
   - ♦ Going into this presentation to dominate or to serve?
   - ♦ Going into it to tell and sell or to listen and see a need and show how my service can fill that need?

5. Focus on **building rapport** with your prospect

6. Operate by the **IR-Theory**:
   I—who you are as an individual
   R—who you are in your role

7. Mix preparation with an **I-will-not-quit** attitude and cap it off with an **I-am-getting-better-with-every-presentation** perspective

> Secrets of the Top Producers
> **"The main thing is how many times you and your team can tell the Pre-Paid Legal story on a daily basis."**
> *-Steve Melia, Encinitas, CA*

Chapter #14 reveals:

- The power of getting referrals

- 3 reasons why people don't give you referrals

- How to call referrals

- How working for superstars can work for you

- Practical steps to getting more referrals than you'll ever need

"Justice For All"

GETTING REFERRALS

"Right now, have the attitude that I'm going to give you $100 cash per person that you know," says top producer Dan Stammen to a new Associate. "Put down 100 to 200 names on this list, plus as many phone numbers and address as you can. Remember that the people you know are interested in Pre-Paid Legal for 1 of 5 reasons:

1. **Career**—dissatisfied with career
2. **Money**—dissatisfied with the amount of money they are making
3. **Fun**—having no fun
4. **Challenge**—wanting a greater challenge
5. **Social**—lacking in social relationships

Empty your brain out on paper. If you put down every name, one person you don't think would ever be interested might trigger you to think of another person who would become a recruit."

Dan then clarifies, "Don't think we are going to 'sign them up' or try to 'sell them something.' We aren't going to do that. All we are going to do is present Pre-Paid Legal to them. It might be for them and it might not, but they might know someone they could refer us to. We are in the sorting business, not the convincing business. All we are going to do is expose them."

The prospect list is vitally important, so

Homerun!
#14.1—Getting 6 to 10 referrals from every member

much so that Dan asks Associates if they mind writing their list of prospects on NCR/carbon paper. Dan then has an immediate copy of 100-200 names. "I'm not leaving my financial future in anyone's hands," he explains. "At $100 a name, these names are extremely valuable, to them and to me."

When the list is complete, Dan then says, "Choose the top 25 people and adopt the attitude that you are borrowing $1 million dollars to start your own business. Who do you want the president, CEO, CFO, or COO of your company to be? Who would you talk to first? Think about recruiting the most successful, aggressive people you know for this opportunity. Then you go down from there."

Then Dan and/or the new Associate begin to contact these top 25 individuals, many of whom become new Associates themselves.

From referrals to recruits and/or members

Though everyone is a potential member, not everyone is a potential recruit. That is why Dan Stammen asks the Associate to choose the top 25. Many great recruits have come from this referral process.

Referrals are similar to centers of influence in that you are borrowing the influence and trust of the person who referred you, you are getting a good reception because you are being respected because of the person who referred you, it saves you time because you are using their leverage, and it helps your own attitude because you aren't talking to a stranger. You are "borrowing" the relationship the person and the referral have.

The biggest difference is that referrals usually come from people who are already Pre-Paid Legal members. This makes their referral all the more powerful because they can talk from experience (i.e. "John, you remember all the trouble I've been having with the phone company? Well, I had my attorney write them a letter on my behalf and two days later the issue was resolved! You need to look at this service...").

Since everyone knows at least 100 other people, it is entirely possible to move from referral to referral—and that is what many top producers do!

3 reasons why people don't give you referrals

All excuses being equal, there are only three reasons why people don't give you referrals. The first is the most common excuse and pertains to you, the second and third pertain to the other individual:

#1—the "I forgot to ask" excuse

Why wouldn't you ask for referrals? Maybe it's because you don't know a referral-request presentation, maybe you forget to ask, or maybe you are afraid (fear of rejection, pride, etc.). The answer is to learn a referral-request presentation (i.e. – "It's been my experience that the more people use their Pre-Paid Legal membership, the more they like it. Who do you know who would also benefit from this service?"), make yourself notes to remember to ask for referrals, or use affirmations to change the way you think to get over your fear. Then ask for as many referrals as you can get. Simply asking for referrals will work 98% of the time.

Getting referrals

#2—the "I don't know anyone" excuse

This mental block of suddenly forgetting all their friends can be quickly remedied: Ask a question to which the answer is a name. For example, "Did you golf this week—who was in your foursome? Who did you go to lunch with this week? Who mows your lawn? Who's your best supplier?" Asking these types of questions will overcome the mental block and give you the names you need.

#3—the conscientious objector excuse

This person, with a little indignation, says, "I don't give referrals" or "I don't know what kind of results I'm going to get." The answer is to divert the focus. Instead of the focus being referrals, change it to introductions. "I just want you to introduce me to someone who I will approach in the same professional manner that I contacted you. If your best customer came in the door, you probably would introduce me to them. That is all I want you to do. I'm not asking you to recommend the service/opportunity, just for you to introduce me to another person." Then ask who they know (same as above).

How to call referrals

When you do get referrals, one of the best ways to present Pre-Paid Legal is through a 3-way call. For example, the Associate might call the person and say, "Hi Fran, this is Jennie, I've come across something that is absolutely incredible and I've got a gentleman I'm working with. He's very successful with this NYSE company and I'd like him to spend a few minutes on the phone with you. Let me call him and see if he is available."

The Associate then 3-ways into you and you tell the referral a little about Pre-Paid Legal, then invite the referral to a PBR, local meeting, or executive luncheon/breakfast if local or you offer to send him or her a CD, video, or audio if long-distance. You make the exposure, let the tools do the presenting, and all the while your Associate is learning how to do what you just did.

You can also call your referrals by yourself. You might say something to the effect of, as Dan Stammen offers:

> Hello, is Fran in? Hi Fran, my name is Dan Stammen. Fran, we haven't been formally introduced, but we have a mutual friend (associate, acquaintance, etc.) Jennie Smith. Jennie and I are working on a project together and she asked me to give you a call.

> So Fran, I'm just curious how you know Jennie? (Get them talking.) Jennie said you were in the _____ business and she spoke very highly of you. Fran, are all the good things she said about you true?

> The reason for the call is that she was curious if you would be willing to keep an open mind and take an objective look at a NYSE listed company that is very unique and exploding throughout North America. Is that fair enough? (Then you lead into a recorded message, mail a CD/Video, etc.)

This is short, sweet, and professional. The bottom line is that the 25 referrals you received from an Associate have great potential because they are their top-25. If four Associates gave you their top-25 prospects, you would have 100 referrals that would be better than any 100 prospects from any one single person. **Referrals are condensed premium individuals, and you want those referrals!**

How to get the "I'm too busy" superstars to give you referrals

It is inevitable that you will find, if you don't know them already, several individuals who would be phenomenal in the business, but they just don't have the time. What should you do with them? The most common approach is to try to slowly and surely recruit them into the business by talking with them, giving them more information, and keeping them up to date about your success in Pre-Paid Legal.

> Secrets of the Top Producers
> "I'm more interested in the people you know and the people they know than I am in my own prospect list."
> -Dan Stammen, Plano, TX

This works with some individuals, but the process is slow even if it is successful. Dan Stammen takes a different approach, one that is focused on getting referrals from these key individuals:

The honest intro

After trying unsuccessfully a couple times to get someone (Bob, in this case) into my business, I'll say, "Bob, you looked at Pre-Paid Legal and decided that it's a good product but you don't have the time." He says, "Absolutely right!" I say, "What if there was a way to use your contacts and credibility and my experience and knowledge and have me involved working for you for free?"

Bob says, "What do you mean?"

Nothing to lose and everything to gain

I say, "Bob, I guarantee you know 8 to 10 key people who would be phenomenal at this business, but you don't have time to recruit them. I want you to take a position with me and sign up in Pre-Paid Legal. We'll sit down and come up with 10, maybe 20, key individuals and I'll call them—I promise I won't embarrass you—and I'll tell them exactly what I told you. If in fact they do get involved in the business, I'll sign them up under you. I can't promise you anything, but 3-6 months down the road, you might be making an extra $500 - $5000 a month off of my time and effort and your contacts and credibility that you aren't using anyway. If you think about it, you have nothing to lose and everything to gain."

When Bob agrees, I get his list and again I'm in a warm market. I take Bob's names and say to Bob, "I know you don't have time to work this business, but I'd like to try to convince you to try to work this business one evening. By that I mean you having a Private Business Reception either in your home or in my home and we'll see if we can't invite out 20-30 people at once. I'll come in and do the presentation with my tools, sales aids, etc. and we'll see what happens. If I sign up 3 or 4 people, I'll start working with them and you can go back to corporate America and you can do whatever you want.

(If Bob doesn't want to do anything more than give me his list of names, that is fine. I'll go through the list myself.)

Burning the fire down below!

After Bob's PBR, things begin to get fun. For example, one person (Brad) becomes an Associate and might turn me on to 20 more people. Of those 20, Jack is ready to go and immediately recommends Mary who quickly signs up. She sends me to Karen who wants to start selling memberships right away. The fact is, I'm starting to make some sales under Bob.

Then I'll call Bob back and say, "You aren't going to believe what's happening. This individual named Karen just signed up 3 people this week in the business, she sold 5 memberships, and she has 3 people coming to a meeting next week. She is really taking off!"

Bob says, "Well, who is Karen?"

I'll say, "Oh, I forgot to tell you. I got Karen's name from Mary and she's doing well in the business."

"Well that's great, but I have to go," Bob says.

"Oh, I forgot to tell you. I got Mary's name from Jack and Jack's name from your friend Brad who you had me call. Thus far, you have 8 people in your group and you've sold 15 memberships. If you can come out this Thursday night, they would like to meet you."

> **Homerun!**
> #14.2—Learning how to "burn a fire down below"

Getting referrals

When Bob comes to the meeting, I introduce him. The people come up and thank him for introducing me to them, thank him for recommending them, etc. They are all excited. Bob says to me, "Let's have lunch together. How did all this happen? I have more people to recommend to you."

It's called "burning a fire down below."

The percentage of people to join up at this point is very high because they have too much to lose. Someone like Bob, Dan is quick to point out, "is better and can get more done than many of the other people on my list combined!" That is the power of tapping into these quality "I'm too busy" people's referral lists. In fact, Dan used to work for another company that did 35 million dollars in business, *but over half of that came from warm lists like this from people who didn't have time to work the business!*

These superstars who are too busy are similar in many respects to Centers of Influence, except that these superstars are also in the business with you. Some become more actively involved than others, but according to Dan, even those who never make a phone call are making anywhere from $500 a month to $6000 a month!

The long-term goal of using these referrals is to find people who will make the time to be actively involved in Pre-Paid Legal for themselves, thus freeing up more of your time.

The added benefit of asking for referrals

Asking for referrals and then following up on those leads will obviously mean more sales and more recruits, and that is great! There is, however, one additional benefit of asking for referrals that will do more to build your business than almost anything else. *It is the fact that your new Associates are watching and learning as you get referrals*.

A lot of people make the mistake of "tell, tell, tell, tell" when it comes to teaching their new Associates how to succeed in Pre-Paid Legal. They tell somebody where to go, they tell them what to say, they tell them how to act, and they tell them what to do.

The fact is people will do what you **show** them,

> Secrets of the Top Producers
>
> "I don't encourage advertising with ads, flyers, etc., until you have established a certain level of income. Until then, master the basics of getting referrals, face to face presentations, etc."
>
> *-Ed Parker, Flower Mound, TX*

not what you **tell** them. That is why top producers take the time to walk new Associates through the Game Plan interview, setting goals, Plan of Action, listing of prospects, ordering tools, etc. Each of these areas is vitally important and can best be explained by watching and seeing how it's done.

The answer is in the "tell, show, try, do" approach and it is to everyone's benefit—yours and theirs—that they know how to do what they need to do to succeed. Getting referrals is one of those secrets to success, so it is important that they know how to do it. As you ask new Associates for referrals, they are watching and learning. When you qualify the leads by asking what they do, how much they make, how long have they lived there, what their needs are, etc., they are again learning. Then when you help them with their new Associates, the cycle is complete.

Your new Associates have learned by doing and are ready to launch out on their own. That is where growth really begins to become evident!

Speed of exposure + the right people

If I am exposing 20 people a week to Pre-Paid Legal and you are exposing 100, you will make more money. Combine that with someone's top 20 or 25 individuals and you will have a very receptive audience and your sales and number of recruits will be much higher. "The easiest way to build your business is through your personal contacts and referrals," Dan concludes, "because you get the least amount of resistance."

This makes getting referrals all the more important. The speed of exposures is vitally important, but when you add in the right qualified people, you are in business! Consider for a minute that you are able to get 6 good referrals from everyone who buys a membership and on average 2 out of 6 new referrals become members. It wouldn't take long before you had a list that was far too big for you to handle.

The math: 1 member = 6 referrals (resulting in 2 new members),
2 new members = 12 referrals,
4 new members = 24 referrals,
8 members = 48 referrals,
16 members = 96 referrals,
32 members = 192 referrals,
64 members = 384 referrals,
128 members = 768 referrals,
256 members = 1536 referrals,
512 members = 3072 referrals,
and on and on...

Getting referrals

And this doesn't even count those who become recruits! With new Associates working with you and getting referrals themselves, you are able to multiply your efforts thousands of times over!

Getting referrals

Steps To Ensure Personal Success
Chapter #14

1. **Always get referrals** from anyone you can

2. **Understand** the 3 reasons why you aren't given referrals:
   a) The "I forgot to ask" excuse
   b) The "I don't know anyone" excuse
   c) The conscientious objector excuse
   and have the answers ready!

3. **Know how to call referrals** with or without the person who made the referral

4. Learn how to "**burn the fire down below**" with superstars who don't have time for Pre-Paid Legal

5. Recognize that the **long-term goal of using referrals** is to find Associates who will actively work the business for themselves

6. Train your new Associates through the "**tell, show, try, do**" approach to continue the referral process

7. **Always get referrals** from anyone you can!

> Secrets of the Top Producers
> "Always use referrals and always teach referrals. You and your team will never run out of prospects."
> -Tom Wood, Ft. Lauderdale, FL

Getting referrals

Chapter #15 reveals:

- The 4 steps of recruiting

- What exposure and follow-up mean to your recruiting

- How to recruit a friend

- The top producers' top 5 tips on recruiting

"Justice For All"

RECRUITING

Tom was told, "You have to recruit up, you have to recruit someone better than yourself," so every time he recruited someone, he told that person the same thing. One day the phone rang; it was a lawyer Tom recruited who happened to be doing business for a man who owned an Fortune 500 company, one of the fastest growing companies in North America. When the lawyer tried to recruit the businessman, he was curtly told, "Show me your big guns."

"I need your help," the lawyer told Tom, so Tom flew down from Boston to West Palm Beach. The businessman's office building was a massive glass structure right on Florida's Intra-coastal Waterway. The glass was from floor to ceiling and you could see all of Palm Beach with the multi-million dollar homes everywhere and the $10 million dollar yachts sailing by his office. On the wall was a picture of this businessman shaking hands with two US Presidents.

"I was totally intimidated," Tom admits. "He sat me down in a low chair and he sat in his high chair behind his desk. He was gray-haired and very distinguished and said to me, 'Listen, I don't have a lot of time, but I've looked into this thing and I'm not really quite sure but why would I want to be involved in this business. Why would I need this?' He was a little brusque and I think he expected someone his age and a little more successful looking."

This businessman had a big center of influence, he was successful, ambitious, and talented, and he was a leader. Tom wanted desperately to recruit him into the business, but what do you say to someone who seems to already have everything?

Tom respectfully said, "You know why you need this...it's because I can go wherever I want, whenever I want, with all of my money at any time with whomever I want, and you can't as long as you stay here. What I have that you will never have is freedom."

The businessman looked at Tom and then said slowly, "Oh my God!" About a month later he sold his business and is today living the life of freedom that he has always wanted through Pre-Paid Legal.

Recruit up

You may not feel comfortable right now being "the big gun," as this businessman put it, but the value of recruiting up remains the same. You also don't have to feel pressure to make such a big presentation at Tom Wood did, now a top producer in Pre-Paid Legal. That is what your sponsor or other top producers are for! They are there for your benefit and will help you recruit up.

> **Homerun!**
> #15.1—Developing a passion
> and an enthusiasm for recruiting

The lawyer who found this businessman could have done a 3-way call and had another person in the business make the presentation. Because a 3rd-party is considered an expert, this is effective with most individuals. With others, you

Recruiting

might want to invite them to a national event so they can get a big picture of Pre-Paid Legal.

Whichever approach you take, keep in mind that the top recruits "get it very quickly," as top producers John and Elizabeth Gardner point out. They understand and have many of the ingredients you are looking for, such as experience in business, sales, management, teamwork, numbers, etc.

Recruiting up is just one of the many areas of recruiting that every Associate needs to learn about, watch in action, and learn to do. Recruiting will do wonders for your team's growth.

Step by step process of recruiting

The process of recruiting is something you have actually already experienced and most likely learned. Here is top producer Brian Carruthers' brief step by step process that will further enforce your ability to recruit:

Step #1—create list of leads from both the warm and cold market. Everyone should start off in his/her warm market (people who know you, love you, and trust you, though they may not respect your business opinion or decision). The cold market is only an add-on to your warm market. Share with them the product, opportunity, or both. I lead with the opportunity, others lead with the product, but it doesn't really matter. It's a systematic approach that you want to run them through; a series of exposures that will help you see if your prospects want to be involved or not.

Step #2—get excited! Before you call, you need to be excited about what you are offering. They will hear it in your voice. People will act more on the height of your enthusiasm than on the depth of your knowledge. It is very important to get excited.

Step #3—call and ask if they are open to the possibilities of a new business. Are they keeping their income options open? If not, then you leave them alone and move on to the next person. If so, give them some information so they can evaluate the service/opportunity properly: a pre-recorded conference call, your website address, a CD-ROM, a video you watch with them, etc. From there, get an interested person on the phone with an "expert"—someone who has been in the business longer than you have and who already has more success than you have. Edify the expert to show credibility in the eyes of your prospect and connect that prospect up with that expert. The expert does the talking, answers the questions, and asks the closing questions.

Step #4—involve your new Associate. Introduce every one of your new Associates to your team, have them be part of some 3-way calls, and help them feel like they are part of something bigger than themselves or just you and them. Have them talk to half a dozen other people on the team and hear their stories. This will encourage, motivate, and inspire them. Also, get the

> **Secrets of the Top Producers**
> "If your sponsor is new to the business as well, keep asking until you find someone's sponsor to help you."
> *-Kelvin Collins, Dallas, TX*

Recruiting

new person plugged into the training process immediately. A new Associate is not expected to learn everything from you. That is where your sponsor and other "experts" come in, along with Pre-Paid Legal's extensive training.

In essence, you take your new Associate through the same process you went through when you entered Pre-Paid Legal. Make it even better! Recruiting is taking more of a managerial role and helping others into the business. Keep in mind that you are not their boss but rather their business partner who desires to see them succeed.

Recruiting at its core: exposure and follow-up

To get people thinking outside of what they are accustomed to, Brian Carruthers asks people, "If you keep doing what you do at your job and you are the best at what you do, 5-10 years from now, will it ever give you the lifestyle, time, financial freedom that you dream about?"

"Not a single person has said that it would," Brian points out. He then asks, "If there is no light at the end of the tunnel, then why keep going down that road?"

> **Secrets of the Top Producers**
> "Time without money is no good and money without time is no good. You need the best of both worlds."
> -Mike Dorsey, Sr., Duluth, GA

With prospects admitting that their current job is not what they need or desire, Brian shares some success stories and lifestyles of some of the top producers, then asks, "If you were the best of the best in Pre-Paid Legal, do you feel Pre-Paid Legal can deliver to you the kind of time, financial freedom and lifestyle that you have always wanted?"

Recruiting

"Absolutely!" is a common response. Brian then states, "If your job won't deliver, why keep going down that road? Put your car on a different path that has a light at the end of the road."

People need a jolt or a nudge in the right direction mentally—a "paradigm shift" as Brian says. It may take a little time through exposure and follow-up, the core ingredients of recruiting, but once prospects make the change, they are unstoppable!

He also makes a point to explain that success in Pre-Paid Legal is not reserved for those who are the best salespeople. "The most successful are those with people skills," he explains, "people who are friendly, who can relate to others, and who can get along with other people."

In short, every new prospect has what it takes to succeed in Pre-Paid Legal!

Why recruiting is the focus

Top producer Frank AuCoin says, "If you have to go to work to make money, you will always have a money monkey on your back. If you don't have assets throwing off money to you, you will always be about 90 days away from being broke. The only way to make one dime is to have an asset, and if you are the asset, you are in trouble. You have to set up assets to throw off money or you will always be in a money crunch."

That very logic is what propelled Brian Carruthers and other top producers to recruit more people into the business with them. Through the efforts of those you recruit, you make overrides that add up to sizeable assets. For example, after a 12-day trip to Europe with his family, Brian came home to find $15,000 had been deposited in his bank account from the activity of those on his team! *That is the power of leveraged income made possible through recruiting!*

"My goal has always been to build a very large team of a lot of people doing a little bit as opposed to a few people doing a lot," says Brian. "This approach works much better than aiming for just a few star performers." With only a few recruits, there is a tendency to expect too much out of them. Your recruits need encouragement, not pressure, so make it your goal to recruit a lot of people.

When it comes down to recruiting those around you, here are 2 common scenarios that may help you:

10 Top Recruiting Affirmations
1. I totally and completely understand the power of multiplication through recruiting.
2. My job description as an Associate says, "Recruit, recruit, recruit!"
3. I love recruiting and begin each day with positive expectancy.
4. I believe that building a great Pre-Paid Legal business will come by recruiting Associates and developing them into leaders.
5. I am a magnet with the power to recruit men and women who share similar values and a passion for my mission with Pre-Paid Legal.
6. Recruiting is the lifeblood of my business.
7. I recruit people into the most rewarding business in this world.
8. I have recruited 100 (500, 1000, 5000, 10,000, whichever is appropriate) individuals for Pre-Paid Legal.
9. I enjoy recruiting more talented, dynamic and experienced people than me.
10. I am an expert in recruiting.

A)—when recruiting a friend

Top producer Kelvin Collins encourages new Associates to take a soft approach with their friends. "If you have friend you've known for a while," he says, "but you are a new recruit, call him or her and say something like, 'I am in a new business. I think it's great...(go through some of the good points about it, but not trying to sell it). I'd like you to meet the individual who helps me in the business and have him explain it to you. He's making a lot of money. It may not be something you are interested in, but I'd like to get your opinion.'"

Such an approach shows respect and takes the focus off of you while not putting your friends in the awkward position of feeling compelled to buy from you. All you really want is their opinion on what you are doing. If they are interested, then you can take them to the next level of exposure.

If they aren't interested after speaking with your 3rd-party expert, listening to a recorded message, or watching a video, etc., then say, as top producer Ken Smith and Patti Ross recommend, "That's fine, I wasn't sure if you would be interested or not. I'll see you next week (or whenever you expect to see them next)."

When they are free to choose, you haven't compromised a friendship, and that is what is most important.

B)—when recruiting a member

After someone buys a membership and you have already asked for and received referrals, you can always say, "If each of these referrals you just gave me ends up buying a membership, I will make ____ dollars (i.e. 8 referrals x $100 = $800). I say that because if you could use the extra money, you could just as easily have your name on the application as mine. Is that something you are interested in?"

If they are interested, then you pull out the Associate application, briefly explain the compensation plan, and maybe watch your Pre-Paid Legal

Recruiting

video, CD-ROM, or online presentation. Then when they fill out the application, you schedule a time with them for their Game Plan interview—and the training process continues.

If they aren't interested, they at least understand the concept. Then you could follow with, "That's fine. I thought that perhaps you might know someone who wants to make between $500 and $5,000 a month from part-time

> **Homerun!**
> #15.2—Understanding that documentation always beats conversation

work. Are any of the referrals you gave me possibly interested or are there other people you know who might be interested?"

Whether they become an Associate or refer you on to others, either way you win!

5 tips for recruiting—*from the top producers*

Recruiting is only beneficial long-term if the individuals remain in the business. Top producer Kathy Aaron says candidly, "I can recruit hundreds of people, but I can't develop all of them. My goal is seeing how many people I can develop because I would rather recruit a few and see them succeed than to try to get a whole lot of people in the business who eventually give up and quit or never grow past their current level."

Developing new recruits includes training, establishing a relationship, creating a friendship, joining them to the team, getting them plugged in, showing them how to make money, helping them see a return on investment as quickly as possible, helping them catch the vision for the service, and more. Recruiting 10 or 20 people in a month may

Recruiting

sound good, but if you can't train them and walk them through the process necessary for their success, then it is just a matter of time before they quit.

That is the responsibility side of recruiting—the other side is the incredible time freedom and financial freedom that comes as the result of recruits who run with the business opportunity that you presented them with. That is where wealth and assets begin to grow, affording you opportunities that you once only dreamed of.

Here are 5 tips from top producers for your initial process of recruiting:

Tip #1—be a people magnet

Associates who are people magnets find recruits everywhere. Why? Because people are drawn to them. Top producer Steve Melia explains it this way: "To attract others, you must be attractive." In other words, work first on yourself—your attitudes, your habits, your discipline, your smile, etc.—then when you meet potential recruits, they will want to work with you.

"Believing in people is amazingly powerful," says top producer Alan Erdlee. Since most

> **Secrets of the Top Producers**
> "People want to know you, like you, and trust you before they do business with you."
> *-Patrick Shaw, Denver, CO*

people don't want to see you succeed, it only follows that most of the people your prospect knows don't want him/her to succeed either.

If you are a people magnet and people can relate to you, they will see themselves doing what you are doing and will gladly join your team.

Recruiting

Tip #2—make the process as easy as possible

One of the most important keys of recruiting is the very process by which you get recruits. If your prospective recruits see that they can do what you are doing, they will be much more likely to join you. Remember that one of their first questions is "Can I do this?" If it's easy, you will have answered their question before they even ask it.

Top producer Patrick Shaw says, "If you can smile and point people to the great tools that are available, you don't have to be the issue. People become the issue when they do all the talking and presenting, and the prospect usually thinks 'I can't do what they are doing.' They quit before they even get started."

The secret is to smile, be excited, and make your presentation with tools (CDs, recorded phone messages, videos, 3rd-party, etc.) that do 90 percent of the work/explanation. *Anyone can do what you are doing—and that is precisely what you want!* That is how you can "massively duplicate and grow a large organization," Patrick states from experience.

But if your approach to getting a recruit cannot be easily replicated, "you will be working yourself to death," as Kelvin Collins says. The easier the recruiting process, the more recruits you are likely to have. (This applies to selling memberships as well.)

Tip #3—recruit to their specialty

The fact of the matter is that not every recruit will want to recruit (or sell memberships) the same way you recruited them into the business. "With new recruits," top producers Frank and Theresa

Recruiting

AuCoin explain, "we try to find their comfort level in the various areas of the business. If they aren't comfortable speaking in front of a group, we aren't going to put them there. Eventually they will be comfortable in all areas so they can teach others to do the same, but initially we aren't going to push them where they don't want to go."

That is what new recruits want to hear! Top producer John Hoffman breaks it down on an individual level with his recruits. He explains how his team operates:

> We take a look at the strengths and interests of the people we choose to work with and put together a business plan that complements the direction they would like to go. For example, a mom who works part-time and wants to make $500 a month will dictate a very different business plan than a new college graduate who wants to build a marketing team with serious duplication and revenue taking place and make $40,000 a month.

When you seek to help your recruits find success through their area of specialty, the bond of teamwork and friendship is unbreakable! That is what you want with every one of your recruits.

Tip #4—get to know your prospects

Every person you meet works in an industry or environment that has unique dynamics. Top producer Steve Fleming has found it highly valuable to ask probing questions to find out what his prospects like and don't like about what they do. "Find out what their unwanted conditions are," Steve explains. "When you know about their unwanted conditions, you can say to other people in

Recruiting

the same industry (real estate for example), 'Don't you hate having to spend Saturdays and Sundays showing homes instead of being at home with your family?'"

How effective is it? Well, Steve has literally thousands of realtors in his business for that very reason—they didn't have their weekends free to spend with their families, but now Pre-Paid Legal has given them the opportunity to do just that! Steve con-

> **Secrets of the Top Producers**
> "New Associates are entrusting themselves, their family, their finances, and their future into the people who recruit them. Our rewards in life are determined by the problems we help solve for others!"
> *-John Hoffman, Knoxville, TN*

cludes, "The only way to get someone to look at a career change is to see that what they have isn't working for them. The 'why not' can be as strong as the 'why' for some people."

By listening and asking questions, you will quickly know what to talk to your prospective recruits about. The more you get to know them, the more they will get to know you, and that further strengthens your team.

Tip #5—recruits need to commit

Top producer Mark Riches takes the recruiting process very seriously. With his new recruits, he asks them to sign a commitment letter and fax him a copy. "It helps me spend time with them when they are that committed," he explains. His commitment letter includes the following commitments:

- ◆ I will be on team's conference call
- ◆ I will attend at least 52 meetings

Recruiting

- ◆ I will attend at least one national event a year
- ◆ I commit to attend all regional trainings and events
- ◆ I set a goal to be in Player's Club each month
- ◆ I will be at least 1 leadership event
- ◆ I commit to this process for 5 years— understanding that the first year is the most effort for smallest return

"The new recruit needs to be told what to do," Mark points out. "They need a framework. It's like a beehive where you put one piece of wax in the hive box and the bees build from there. The Associates build their own business, but I provide the framework."

Part of the commitment required by the new recruit is obviously shouldered by Mark and every Associate who works to recruit others into the business. It will take time to adequately train them, but once the training is done, your recruits will be equipped to succeed. "The secret," Mark says from first-hand experience, "is to set a steady pace to recruit a few people each month,

> **Homerun!**
> #15.3—Letting people become recruits rather than convincing them to do so

train them, and never miss a month. It won't be long before your business begins to explode."

The time to recruit is now!

As you talk to your prospects, keep the marketing plan simple and basic, regardless of how experienced you are in Pre-Paid Legal. What is interesting, says Mark Riches, is that new Associates are at the lowest knowledge level they will ever be just coming into the business while their enthusiasm is at its highest level. What this means is that they are most effective in recruiting at that very moment!

Knowledge on ice will always be outperformed by ignorance on fire. That is because excitement and belief—rather than logic—is what recruits. Education is part of the training process and is vitally important, but it tends to dampen the enthusiasm. "Remember what you know now and tell just that," Mark tells new Associates, "Don't tell the knowledge."

The fact is *it's always time to recruit!* If you are wondering what top producers do, they always keep it simple and they are always recruiting, recruiting, recruiting.

Recruiting

Steps To Ensure Personal Success
Chapter #15

1. **Recruit up**

2. Learn the **4 proven steps to recruiting**:
   #1—create list of both warm and cold market leads
   #2—get excited
   #3—call and ask if they are open to the possibilities of a new business
   #4—involve your new Associate

3. **Create assets** and **leverage your time** through recruiting

4. Be a **people magnet**

5. Make the recruiting process as **easy as possible**

6. **Recruit** to your prospective recruit's specialty

7. **Get to know** your prospects

8. **Be committed** to your recruits

9. **Recruit! Recruit! Recruit!**

Secrets of the Top Producers
"If you don't recruit, 100% of your income is dictated by what you do."
-Brian Carruthers, Rockville, MD

Recruiting

Chapter #16 reveals:

- What duplication should mean to you

- 2 questions your duplication process must always answer

- The top producers' 21 secrets for duplication

- What it really means to focus on duplication

"Justice For All"

Duplicating

Dan said to his new Associate, "If you walk into my office and spend an hour telling me everything I need to know about a membership and I decide to buy it because you answered every question perfectly, you've sold one membership. But if you were to ask if I wanted to make a career change and sell Pre-Paid Legal, I would think, 'There is no way I could do what you just did—it would take me 6 months to learn how to do that!'"

"Instead," Dan continued, "if you walked in my office and said, 'I've got something that is incredible! It's a NYSE company that is exploding, 30 years in business, debt free, and millions in the bank, and by the way, everything you need is on this CD-ROM—let's pop it in your computer and watch a little bit together,' I would be much more likely to get involved."

> **Homerun!**
> #16.1—Understanding duplication and duplicating that understanding

The new Associate was beginning to understand his job is that of being a good pointer toward the tools and the system. Anybody can do that.

Then Dan said, "If at the end of the CD's presentation you say, 'Do you know anyone who wants to make an extra $500 a month or $5000 a month?' I would likely say, 'I sure do—I do!' Why would I respond that way?"

The Associate replied, "Because all I did was talk for a few minutes and pop in a CD that explained the service and opportunity. Anyone can do that!"

"Exactly!" top producer Dan Stammen exclaimed, "And that is what duplication is all about!"

What is duplication?

To put it plainly, **duplication is the secret to your success in Pre-Paid Legal!** Without it, none of the top producers would be in the position they are in today. That is because the foundation of duplication is based on one principle: the law of compounding. (Little wonder why Albert Einstein called compounding the 8th wonder of the world!)

Compounding takes what you have and multiplies it over and over and over and over and over again! What you get is far more than you initially invested. That is how $1000 can become $1,000,000 over time, how 2 people can have thousands in their lineage, and how drops of water can eventually bore a hole through solid granite. **It is also how one person can build a team in Pre-Paid Legal that has thousands of Associates with tens of thousands of membership sales!** This may sound a little too mathematical, but it is a principle that must become an active part of your daily life!

With every Associate, top producer Michael Clouse defines duplication this way: "What I am about to do with you, you must be able to immediately do with the next person you meet with or without my help, whether that person lives across the street, across the town, or across the country."

Top trainer Jeff Olson says it another way, "Whatever you do in Pre-Paid Legal, it has to work 4 or 5 levels below you, 2000 miles away, without you present, with a dud talking to a stud. If what you do violates that, you are out of business."

In other words, if it isn't compounding, it isn't growing. The answer is to plug into what has been proven to work in Pre-Paid Legal and then have your recruits plug into the same system and have their recruits do the same. This is duplication in action and growth is sure to follow.

2 questions that any duplication process must answer

Top producers Ken Smith and Patti Ross follow a tried and proven system. They and their team continually ask two questions:

> *Question #1—Is what I'm about to do to this person something they can do to someone else immediately without me being there?*

Could you contact someone in the next 15 to 30 minutes who had never heard of Pre-Paid Legal or this business opportunity, expose them to what it is, and leave them in the situation where at the end of 30 minutes, they can do exactly what you had just done? That is a powerful question!

Ken points out, "You want to be system-dependent, not people dependent. It's not about remembering the details or being an eloquent salesperson. It's about using the tools: recorded messages, CD-ROMs, web pages, audios, recorded phone messages, etc."

Duplicating

> ***Question #2—Is what I'm about to do to this person something they can do to someone else immediately across the street or across the continent?***

"Regardless of where you live," says Patti, "if you are system-dependent and if you answer those two questions, then you can generate income from virtually anywhere."

How effective is such a system? Ken and Patti had one individual who was successful in his public speaking and in his work, but when it came to Pre-Paid Legal, he did everything by himself. After two years, he had as high at 17 memberships sold in one month in his entire team. After about 90 days of using a proven system, his team jumped to 86 memberships sold in one month!

> Secrets of the Top Producers
> **"We are not only telling Associates how to work the business, but we are creating a relationship."**
> *-Bill Carter, Albuquerque, NM*

People are often a little resistant to plugging into an existing system, but results—membership sales and recruits—have a way of speaking for themselves!

21 secrets for success through duplication

Duplication is really no secret! Rather, it is simply the result of consistently taking the right action steps. And because duplication is really a law of nature, it works just as well for you as it does for the top producers!

Here are 21 of the top producers' secrets to duplication:

Secret #1: start with a relationship

"Your success in this business is going to be directly related to the number of friends that you can make," says top producer Alan Erdlee. "All you need to do is go make friends and the rest will come."

If you or those on your team have a hard time building friendships, having a team spirit and working together will be rather difficult. Alan helps his recruits by explaining how building relationships is fundamental to success in Pre-Paid Legal and how getting educated on how to form lasting relationships is a must. Alan says candidly, "I would probably stick several books under their nose to get them thinking with hopes that they would begin to see the importance of building relationships."

Every top producer has formed meaningful relationships. Top producer Bill Carter's perspective is helpful, "Pre-Paid Legal is a network marketing company—that's how we do business; Pre-Paid Legal is a multi-level marketing company—that's how we get paid; but Pre-Paid Legal is really a relationship business. We should really call it 'relationship marketing.'"

That is why top producers Bill and Annette Hamilton say, "In Pre-Paid Legal, the relationship you form with your Associates is what holds the business together."

Secret #2: help your Associates find success immediately

"If you can show your new Associates a little success up front, that is the secret to getting them hooked," says top producer Mark Riches. "If you can show them small successes early, you will keep

Duplicating

them and they will become leaders." It certainly isn't a free ride, however. Mark has them learn how to define the membership's value and how to make an effective presentation.

Top producer Patrick Shaw says, "We go out and help new Associates get their first 3 or 4 member- ships. When the Associates get their first check within a

> Secrets of the Top Producers
> **"I treat Pre-Paid Legal like the business that it is."**
> *-John Hoffman, Knoxville, TN*

week or two, the first major hurdle of the business has been cleared. They do the same with their new recruits."

Such an approach is simple and replicable— and that is how you multiply.

Secret #3: treat it like a business

Most Associates are part-time in Pre-Paid Legal, while some are full-time. What is important is your attitude, not the number of hours you spend in the business. Granted, those who work full-time should make more than those who work part-time, but what helps make top producers the top produc- ers is the fact that they treat their Pre-Paid Legal business like a business. **They take it seriously.**

Those who take it seriously will enjoy the results of their labor. Top producer Mike Melia explains:

> I have an Associate on our team who worked hard and recruited about 15 people into the business in her first 6 months. Then she got sick with a life-threatening illness. Her team continues to grow, even though she hasn't worked the business in 2 years! She

makes about $6,000 to $9,000 a month. She is an exception to the rule, but the point is that she started right, she got her new Associates plugged in and trained, she had her team at the events, and they all treated it like a business.

Top producer Mark Brown might have said it best when he said, "If you work half as hard in Pre-Paid Legal as you do at your regular job, there is no way you can fail."

Secret #4: don't reinvent the wheel

"The network marketing industry has been around for decades, so you don't have to create anything new," says top producer John Hoffman. "All you need to do is take the same principles of those who are succeeding in Pre-Paid Legal and stick to them."

These principles he is talking about are the basics to the business that anyone can replicate. Always go back to the basics.

Secret #5: begin with the Game Plan interview

Top producer Kathy Aaron says, "You multiply by doing a Game Plan interview with you new Associates." Part of the Game Plan interview is discovering the new recruits' WHY for being in the business. This is vital information for you as the sponsor and for your new Associates.

From there, Kathy focuses on the practical how-to steps of making the business work. She understands clearly that when the WHY is big enough, the HOW will take care of itself.

Secret #6: take responsibility for yourself

When John Hoffman was starting in Pre-Paid Legal, he knew that if he could learn how to market a membership, he could then teach other people to market the membership. That is precisely what he did and is today one of Pre-Paid Legal's top producers. To help set a standard for others, you must be willing to set a standard for yourself. The secret of your future is hidden in your daily routine."

> Secrets of the Top Producers
> **"If it's simple, it's duplicable."**
> -Mike Melia, Atlanta, GA

Top producer Dan Stammen takes a similar approach while working with new recruits. He explains, "I take full responsibility for where I am and where I'm not." He focuses his attention on his recruits' prospect lists because he understands that those 100 to 200 names are like gold to him and his recruits—and he is right!

Secret #7: use the tools

I've seen the absolute best salesmen fail simply because they had a big head; they were proud. Network marketing is about trust, building friendships, and work. Charm may get you a sale, but it won't be of any benefit to the individual you bring into the business.

That is why Pre-Paid Legal's tools are so valuable—anyone can give them out to other people. Mike Melia says, "The more tools you get out there, the more it will duplicate, and the more it duplicates, the more successful you will be."

What's more, when you use the tools, you are the messenger, not the message. Potential recruits will understand this immediately.

Secret #8: believe in your team

"Sometimes you have to believe more in your new Associates than they believe in themselves," says Patrick Shaw. What that means, among other things, is that you are a constant source of encouragement and support to them. Since they are on the learning curve, your wisdom and positive attitude will be like a breath of fresh air.

Spending time with your recruits is also a powerful belief statement. Top producer Steve Melia takes his new recruits to national events. "If their belief factor is huge, they will be mentally

> Secrets of the Top Producers
> "Every time you are productive, you are moving closer to your goals."
> -KC Townes, Universal City, TX

tough," he notes, "but if their belief factor is nothing, they will quit at the first challenge, first "no," or first ounce of disapproval from a friend. By picking them up and taking them to big conferences and big events will increase their belief factor significantly."

Secret #9: remain balanced as you monitor your team's progress

"If you only recruit and don't pay attention to anyone, the business will fail," top producer Michael Dorsey points out. "And if you only manage and don't recruit, the business will fail also." The secret is to be balanced between building and managing, which for most Associates is about 80% recruiting/presenting and 20% managing.

Duplicating

When a new Associate says, "I can't sell a membership," top producer Frank AuCoin immediately replies, "Ok, sell me the membership. Tell me the 5 Titles and I'll tell you if I'll buy it when you get done."

It usually takes only a few seconds to discover that the individual hasn't taken the time to learn the 5 Titles, the company history, or the compensation plan. "You can't do business if you don't know those 3 things and can't explain them," says Frank. "That's all there is to the business!"

Other recruits who are struggling are often not plugged into Pre-Paid Legal's communication systems, listening in on leadership calls, attending the local events, using the tools, etc. Frank monitors his team's progress so he can help them progress to the next level, but he spends the majority of his time working with those who don't **need** his help.

Secret #10: help prepare your new Associates' Plan of Action

"I make it a point that when the new recruits leave the Game Plan interview with me, they know what their next step is," says top producer Bill Carter. He helps them form their Plan of Action. They know what approach, what tools, and what exposure—and they are ready to follow up on their Plan of Action.

At that point, the new Associates are thinking, "I'm ready to go to work and I know exactly what I need to do. I need to get the tools into my prospect's hands and then set up a 3-way call with my sponsor and my prospect."

It's simple and it's duplicable, and that is what you want your new Associates to think!

Secret #11: use On the Job Training (OJT)

Of all the different forms of trainings, Mark Riches sees OJT as the most effective. This is where the new Associate follows the sponsor around, watching how to make a sale, how to get referrals, and even how to handle rejection.

"We do 3-way calls with the top 10 prospects if the Associates are long-distance," he explains. "That's not quite as effective since you aren't spending time in the car and being with them for half a day, but it still works." What is important is that your new recruits are watching and listening because we learn the best by showing and doing rather than by listening and reading.

Secret #12: sell them on the team

We all want to belong. Ken Smith and Patti Ross understand this. "We sell new Associates on the team and not on ourselves," they say. "We show them the other people on the team who have succeeded." Ken and Patti's perspective is that the network in network marketing is the team on the inside of Associates, not the prospects on the outside.

What does this mean? It means that "each of the team players is available to the new Associates," Ken explains. When a prospect who owns a lot of real estate and shopping centers showed interest in becoming an Associate, his sponsor called top producer Brian Carruthers, whose family is very successful in real estate, and Brian endorsed Pre-Paid Legal. The prospect became an Associate right away.

"If you don't use the tool of the team you have, you miss out," Ken concludes.

Secret #13: track your growth

When you track your progress, you know if you are on target with your Plan of Action and goals in general. The Pre-Paid Legal *Success Planner*, the "nucleus of the system," as Michael Clouse calls it, is designed to help you track your progress from month to month.

It also helps you remain organized and efficient with your time.

> **Homerun!**
> #16.2—Finding those people who will match your level of energy and effort

Successful people have developed a habit of doing what the unsuccessful do not do, and that includes making calls, getting leads, getting referrals, making recruits, setting goals, etc. Until you can track your progress, you can't manage it.

Secret #14: run on 90-day cycles

Mike Melia says, "We run the business in 90-day cycles, from one national event to the next." He asks those in his team, "Where do you want to be by the next event?" They then make 90 or 120-day goals and then back that goal up and work from there.

It's like making a fresh Plan of Action every quarter. "The weekly meetings and weekly leadership calls keeps it all regular," Mike adds. The secret is that he is keeping his team working toward relevant attainable goals that have a definite time frame for their attainment. That is powerful!

Secret #15: identify your leaders and build a team

"The way they build a massive organization is to identify your leaders and teach them to teach so that you can duplicate the process," says top producer Larry Smith. Finding leaders is easy. Look for people who:

- ♦ are excited
- ♦ love teamwork
- ♦ want to learn
- ♦ are willing to pay the price
- ♦ are not willing to quit!

With these Associates, spend most of your time. Build a team with them because they are the ones who will make the most impact—and they are the ones who will reach their dreams with you!

Secret #16: attend events

It's a proven fact that Associates who have attended previous conventions and major events significantly outperform those who do not attend. It is estimated that those Associates who attend both annual major events will increase their annual sales by an average of 50 percent more than if they had not attended!

In other words, do whatever you have to do to get to the next major event—and take your new

> **Secrets of the Top Producers**
> "If someone is doing something that is working successfully but that is not duplicable, I highly recommend that they eliminate it."
> -Craig Hepner, Newport Beach, CA

Associates with you! Top trainer Jeff Olson adds, "The corporate event is where you get your long-dis-

Duplicating

tance group together. Plan for it, then get together before, after, and during it."

Smaller weekly events can be equally as valuable, especially since they help keep your Associates' passion and excitement levels high.

Secret #17: let the system do most of the training

"You are typically not the person who does the training with new Associates," says top producer Brian Carruthers. "You as the sponsor should do the Game Plan interview with them, develop a Plan of Action, establish their goals, etc., but the key is to understand that if you become the issue and expect them to learn from you and you alone, you are not going to have much success because you don't know enough to teach it all."

The fact is no top producer will put himself or herself in the position of "knowing it all." When you do this, you become the center of attention and your ability to duplicate is drastically reduced.

Brian continues, "I encourage everyone to plug into the system and let the system do 90% of the work. Let those who have already been there and done that be the ones in front of the room or on conference calls. New Associates can learn from the best of the best exactly what to do, what to say, etc. You are the messenger, not the message."

Secret #18: follow a presentation system that duplicates

"About 80% of the training a person needs will be done by the time they sign their paperwork to become an Associate," says Patti Ross, "*if* they are using a predictable and repeatable system."

With this type of system, a new recruit is, for example, introduced to the business through watching a video, followed-up by a 3-way call with a 3rd-party expert, and then invited to a local event where he or she becomes an Associate.

When that new Associate signs the Associate Membership, he or she is virtually ready to go out and use the same "predictable and repeatable system." This is also beneficial because the new Associate wasn't exposed to the business through one avenue, then told to use another when recruiting. When it's all the same, there is much less confusion and much more duplication, which is exactly what you want!

Secret #19: take consistent daily action

Top producer Dave Savula's "2 a day and one weekly meeting" has been a formula for many people's success. What it comes down to is consistent daily activity, such as mailing out one long-distance package every day, calling 2 new prospects on the phone

> **Secrets of the Top Producers**
> "I expose 1 to 3 people a day and send out one long-distance packet a week and go to the meetings, that is about as far as I look on a daily basis."
> *-Mark Brown, Weatherford, TX*

every day, or talking to a businessperson every day during your lunch break.

Jeff Olson adds one thing: "Do the things you ask others to do." Not only is that good for your team's growth, but it is also good for your own personal business success.

Secret #20: keep it simple

Dan Stammen reduces the business plan for his new Associates down to this:

> 1-you get people to take a look
> 2-you get it to make sense
> 3-you get them to decide
> 4-you help those who say "yes" to get results

That's it! Patrick Shaw says, "Success in Pre-Paid Legal is simple: learn how to sell a membership, invite/expose people to the opportunity, and learn how to get the new person started right." When you keep the simplicity of the process it mind, it will help you and everyone you recruit into the business.

Secret #21: stay focused on what duplicates

Duplication requires constant attention. If we get off track and start using a successful approach that is not duplicable, we are short-circuiting our own success. As Dave Savula says, "You are either in focus or you are out of focus—there is no in-between." We must remain intensely focused on what duplicates.

"There are too many ways in Pre-Paid Legal that work to choose only one method," says Michael Clouse. "We have to stop asking 'Will it work?' and start asking 'Will it duplicate?'" Everything will work, though it might not work very well, much less be worth duplicating.

One way to test if the method you are using is duplicable is to apply top producers John and Elizabeth Gardner's logic to it: "If you can't teach it, don't do it!" For something to duplicate, it follows that you must be able to teach it, and if you can teach it, it also stands to reason that hundreds, even thousands of other people could be teaching or learning how to do it as well!

> Secrets of the Top Producers
> **"Learn, teach, and then teach others to teach."**
> -Eric Worre, Eden Prairie, MN

Whichever method you choose for selling memberships and recruiting others into the business, make sure it is a proven system that duplicates. Only through such a method will you find success in Pre-Paid Legal.

Steps To Ensure Personal Success
Chapter #16

1. Understand the **law of compounding**

2. Be **system-dependent**, not people dependent

3. Learn, teach, and then **teach others to teach**

4. Practice the following **21 secrets to duplication**:

#1: start with a relationship
#2: help your Associates find success immediately
#3: treat it like a business
#4: don't reinvent the wheel
#5: begin with the Game Plan interview
#6: take responsibility for yourself
#7: use the tools
#8: believe in your team
#9: remain balanced as you monitor your team's progress
#10: help prepare your new Associates' Plan of Action
#11: use On the Job Training (OJT)
#12: sell them on the team
#13: track your growth
#14: run on 90-day cycles
#15: identify your leaders and build a team
#16: attend events
#17: let the system do most of the training
#18: follow a presentation system that duplicates
#19: take consistent daily action
#20: keep it simple
#21: stay focused on what duplicates

> Secrets of the Top Producers
> "Every top producer in Pre-Paid Legal got there step by step. You have the same opportunity. My advice to you is simple: copy them."
> -Paul J. Meyer, Waco, TX

Conclusion

Top producer Patrick Shaw sums it up when he says, "The only thing that matters is being in the game a year from now, having desire, and being teachable—and those are just choices."

It is all about choices, from beginning to end. The top producers choose every day to stick with the proven system for success in Pre-Paid Legal. You have their proven system in front of you—you now know exactly where to start, what to do, and how to do it. You know everything you need to know to be successful in Pre Paid Legal.

The only question remaining is this: all the people you know and the people they know who would benefit by the Pre Paid Legal service and/or opportunity—***will you make the advance commissions, overrides, and residual income or will someone else?***

That too is a choice.

Reference Information for Pre-Paid Legal

Pre-Paid Legal Services, Inc.

PO Box 1379 Ada, OK 74821 (*new business and resubmitted or returned business*)

PO Box 2629 Ada, OK 74821 or fax: 580-636-7496 (*bank changes and membership reinstatements*)

PO Box 145 Ada, OK 74821 (*miscellaneous*)

PPL Corporate Web Site: www.prepaidlegal.com

Marketing:

Marketing Services (*for all your business questions*): 580-436-7424

Marketing Services fax: 580-436-7496

Marketing Services email: marketingservices@pplsi.com

Licensing questions: 580-436-7424 or licensing@pplsi.com

Corporate Communications Fax (*for ad approvals*): 580-421-6305

Fast Start to Success Tabletop Training Completion Forms (*located at end of* Fast Start to Success *booklet*): 580-436-7496

Stock Information: 800-654-7757, Option 3

Customer Care Services:

Customer Care (*membership questions*): 800-654-7757

Customer Care Fax (*member bank & address changes*): 580-436-7565

Legal Shield (*in case of detainment*): 877-825-3797 (toll-free)

Group Marketing:

PO Box 2479, Ada, OK 74820

Group Questions (*Incl. Group Seminar & Small Business Seminar registration*): 580-421-6326, fax (*for questions and/or seminar registration*): 580-421-6311

Group Marketing email: groupmarketing@pplsi.com

Group Marketing conference call (*every Monday 9 a.m. EST*): 412-858-5200 or 1-888-379-9511)

PPL Interactive Voice Response (IVR) System:

Call 800-699-9004, enter your Associate number and PIN#, then choose from the following options:

> Option 1—Recent updates
> Option 2—Main Menu
>> Push 1 for Associate information
>> Push 2 for Fax-on-Demand
>> Push 3 for Web Support

Supply orders:

Marketing services: phone orders: 580-436-7424 (option 3), fax orders: 580-436-7496

Video*Plus* orders & information: 800-388-3884, fax orders: 940-497-9799

Video*Plus* orders online: www.ppltools-videoplus.com

Communication:

Televox Voice Response System customer service: 888-871-4951, fax: 888-266-6897

Member Retention Services:

Integrity Resource Management: 1-888-272-0986 or www.integrity4you.com

Federal Express:

Overnights (only by FedEx) to: 321 East Main Street, Ada, OK 74821

To open a FedEx account (free), order pre-printed labels & envelopes, request pickup, track shipments: phone 800-GO-FEDEX (800-463-3339) or online at: www.fedex.com

Business Card and Letterhead

1) Pre-Paid Legal: 321 E. Main Ada, OK 74820 or 1-580-436-7424
2) Personal Image Concepts: P.O. Box 700 Troutdale, OR 97060-9700 or 1-503-492-0397 or http://www.piconcepts.com/ppl
3) JFA Print Services: 1-866-532-6654 (toll free) or www.jfaonline.com
4) The Print Centre: #108, 19915-64 Avenue Langley, BC V2Y 1G9 Canada or 604-533-2636, fax: 604-533-6552

(NOTE: All business cards must be purchased from one of the above mentioned licensed vendors.)

Apparel

Kerma's Kreations: 800-757-1193 or www.kermas.com
Cettas Specialties: 816-741-2239 or www.cettas.com

Audios, Videos, and Presentation tools:

Video*Plus*: 800-388-3884 or www.ppltools-videoplus.com

Banners and Signs:

Fast Signs: 405-942-0317 or www.pplfastsigns.com

Presentation Boards:

JB's Presentations: 219-663-0900, ext. 209 or www.jbspresentations.com

Badges, Trophies, and Statues:

Justice Galleries: 417-882-7927
Trophies & More: 740-383-1945

About the authors:

Paul J. Meyer knows marketing inside and out, from top to bottom, forward and backward with over 50 years of experience. Beginning at age 19, he become the leading income earner and top producer in two of the largest US insurance agencies.

He went on to form Success Motivation Institute and has authored 24 major programs on sales, motivation, goal setting, management, and leadership development with a combined sales in 60 countries in 20 languages of more than 2 billion dollars, more than any other author in history. He is considered by many to be the founder of the personal development industry.

His recent books include *Chicken Soup for the Golden Soul*, which was on the *New York Times* best-seller list for many months, and *Unlocking Your Legacy*, which outlines 25 of his top secrets for success.

Kevin Rhea is President of L-K Marketing Group, one of the leading organizations in Pre-Paid Legal. Kevin is responsible for managing and overseeing the day-to-day operations, growth, stability, and future progress of L-K Marketing. He and the leaders of L-K Marketing have put together an impressive track record of success in Pre-Paid Legal.

In 2001, L-K Marketing was recognized as a $1 Million Income Earner. Kevin is quick to point out that the credit goes directly to the many top producers in L-K Marketing. What really motivates Kevin is seeing the leaders on the team achieve their goals and receive recognition for their success in Pre-Paid Legal.

Brian Mast, formerly the managing editor for a business magazine, is an editor and author of *How to manage a million dollars or less* and *Profiles of Success.* He is also an Independent Associate with one of the fastest growing companies on the New York Stock Exchange: Pre-Paid Legal Services, Inc.

How to order more copies of *Success in Pre-Paid Legal:*

Single copies and bulk orders can be made through Video*Plus*:

◆ Order online at: www.ppltools-videoplus.com
◆ Phone orders: 1-800-388-3884
◆ Fax orders: 1-940-497-9799

Mail orders to:
Video*Plus* Inc.
200 Swisher Road
Lake Dallas, TX 75065

Your Game Plan interview Checklist:

❑ 1) Set the appointment with your sponsor

❑ 2) Read the *Fast Start to Success* booklet and listen to the audio tape

❑ 3) Make your initial list of 100 prospects

❑ 4) Write down your one to five year goals

❑ 5) Make it a point not to talk to anyone about Pre-Paid Legal just yet

❑ 6) Prioritize your list of 100-200 names

❑ 7) Get on the communication systems for Pre-Paid Legal

❑ 8) Buy the Pre-Paid Legal *Success Planner*

❑ 9) Schedule to attend the next Fast Start Classroom Training in your area

❑10) Make a 1-year commitment to your success in Pre-Paid Legal

Today's Date

(Your Sponsor's Name)
(Your Sponsor's Address)
(Your Sponsor's City, State, Zip)

Dear (Your Sponsor's Name):

(Body of your letter here.)

I will be here, still actively involved in the process of building my Pre-Paid Legal business, 1 (or 5) year(s) from now.

Over the next 1 (or 5) year(s) I will build my business to the _____ level.

I will remain coachable, teachable, and willing to learn.

The reason I became involved with Pre-Paid Legal is that I want ...

I am framing this letter, and will be placing it in my _____ where I can view it daily. To ensure my success, I am also committing publicly by sending additional copies of this letter, all with my original signature, to those listed below.

Sincerely,

(Your Original Signature)

(Your Full Name)

CC: Mr. Harland Stonecipher
        Mr. Wilburn Smith
        (Your Upline Executive Director)
        (Your Upline Platinum Executive Director)

Whatever you vividly imagine, ardently desire, sincerely believe, and enthusiastically act upon must inevitably come to pass.

-Paul J. Meyer